Work

Work

Decoding Work for the Neurodiverse Worker

Andrew Schlegelmilch, Ph.D.

First published in 2022
by Sixth City Press.

Cleveland, OH

Edited by Pat Schlegelmilch

Front cover image source: Shutterstock. The front cover is for illustrative purposes only, and any person featured is a model.

Thank you to my readers, Ed Myracle and Carolyn Rodecker

Version 1.3

Dedication

This book is dedicated to my dad, who taught me how to work. He trained me, supervised me, then gave me responsibility.

Contents

Introduction

You have Autism Spectrum Disorder or some related diagnosis, disability, or distinction. You have likely discovered that ASD is a big part of your life, but it hardly defines you. Many of you are working, some in careers. Many of you are parents. Many of you are spouses. Many of you are caretakers, decision-makers, politicians, or first responders. Many of you volunteer some of your time.

The scope of this book is broad, considering I am writing to a group of people who have autism and are between the ages of 18 and 64. You are in your working, parenting, and coupling years. Traditionally, many also consider these years to be your most productive years.

Some of you received your autism diagnosis at the age of two, and some of you just found out a couple of days ago. Those diagnosed at two received an "early diagnosis." Early childhood is more typical for a regular diagnosis, and after that is a late diagnosis. Any diagnosis after the age of 18 is considered a "very late diagnosis," and it seems more and more people are receiving this very late diagnosis, which is a primary reason for the writing of this book.

I am working with more and more adults receiving an autism diagnosis after they were married and had children, after being promoted way high up in a huge corporation, or after their first cardiac arrest. They found themselves in situations where they needed better communication skills, more effective organizational skills, or better self-help skills. They or someone around them realized a fundamental gap between their current skill set that got them into that place and the skills they would need to get through it. In conversations with my clients, it is not uncommon to find elaborate and intricate processes to manage the demands of daily living or careers, but limited information or training on how to manage other, more esoteric situations. For instance, what happens when you are so good at your job that you are promoted into a management position and have no idea how to manage the people under you? What happens when your loving child suddenly wants nothing to do with you, and the only cause you can determine is that he became a teenager? What happens when you have a significant health event, and doctors recommend you change everything about how you spend your time?

This book is a primer on how to be an adult in real-time. For years I have written about preparing for adulthood, but there are realities to being an adult that most people don't even think about until they are adults. Some realities can't be addressed until one becomes an adult. Even parents training their children for adulthood don't think about most of the practical, day-to-day decisions they have to make just to keep from having a terrible day.

In addition, this book will attempt to add an element of problem-solving to the mix. Most "how-to" books about children and adolescents on the spectrum consider that most children (with or without autism) cannot effectively problem-solve. Problem-solving is a skill dependent on brain development, much like algebra. It requires executive functioning skills and abilities to use abstract reasoning. Children can be taught the "Four Steps of Problem Solving" and memorize the steps for effective recitation, but using those skills flexibly and in real-time is a task better suited for adults. I have been able to teach practical problem-solving skills to adults on the spectrum, whereas I have had very little success doing so with children. With problem-solving skills, not all situations that pose a problem require a rigid or scripted answer from a teacher.

This book aims to strike a nice balance between describing the demands of situations and their scripted solutions and teaching the skills of problem-solving and innovating in these situations. It would make sense that the abilities and qualities that got you this far could be activated to bring you the rest of the way. I have found that insight and guidance from me and other experts, combined with intention and hard work from my clients, is what it takes to move forward.

Upon reflection, I have found that my adult clients influence how I live my life. So I hope to take the best of what I have learned from my clients and add it to this book. What follows are the most concise and practical descriptions and the best advice on how to work.

Chapter 1

What is the format of work life?

Before getting a job, most people have little appreciation for work life. They might know that their mom or dad goes to work and comes home in the evening. People on TV have jobs. Work is pretty standard, but it can be tough to differentiate work from not-work for most people before they have experienced it. Inability to distinguish work and not-work is a problem because most people must work.

The US established child labor laws in the early part of the 20th century. At that time, most children went to school rather than work. The consensus was that it was unjust to make children work. Children should instead learn about how to work before they work. This learning, however, primarily includes teaching the general and specific skills necessary for doing a job, such as reading and math. Our education system has traditionally done an inferior job teaching people how to work or what employers and co-workers expect of them in the "workplace."

To their credit, educators have done excellent work making school look like a job. Most people have heard it said to school-age children that going to school was their "job" and they should treat it that way. However, most children that attend school for any number of years may have some sense of the structure of the work world, but are missing some essential pieces of information. Consequently, most of my vocational support and training work entails describing the workplace structure and the workplace behaviors that jobs require.

Often I get the most mileage out of comparing and contrasting work and school.

Hierarchy

All of society is a hierarchical system of some kind. Indeed, both work and school are hierarchical systems. There are people on top and people down below. In school, the people on the top are teachers and administrators, and the people down below are the students. School also cleverly creates a hierarchy among students through assigning grade levels and terms such as "upperclassmen" and "under (not, lower) classmen." The discussion of the hierarchy function is outside the scope of this chapter. Suffice to say, it is functional and thus exists, and it exists and therefore must serve some use. Many future workers who get used to the hierarchical school system have a basic understanding of how the hierarchy will function in the work world. However, the school experience is insufficient to fully prepare the young adult for the work world hierarchy.

Schools employ a fixed and progressive hierarchy. Students move up the student hierarchy at one notch a year (by grade level). Teachers will always remain above the students and administrators (in most cases) above the teachers. Even school "staff," such as bus drivers, custodians, secretaries, and the like, are above the students in the hierarchy because they are adults. Adults bring some of their status from society into the workplace. Students can never rise above adults in the school hierarchy. I should also point out that for some people in the hierarchy in the school building (the students), the system is school, but for others (the adults), the system is work. Interestingly, even if a student turns 18 while a student, they remain below the other adults present because it's their workplace. The ultimate determination of this hierarchy is this stringent rule around the reason for being in the school building.

Whereas age defines the school hierarchy, ability and the worker's relative value to the company determines the work environment hierarchy. Brighter or more competent students will never rise above teachers, but more competent employees can undoubtedly rise above their managers. Indeed, it is not uncommon for the person hired after you to be promoted before you, make more money than you, or even become your manager or boss. The work world is primarily a meritocracy where employees are assigned values based on many things, but ultimately by their merit. The higher the value, the higher in the hierarchy one can climb.

What does this mean for training the school child to be competent in the workplace hierarchy? The applications of this notion of meritocracy are probably unlimited. Primarily, however, instead of rising in the hierarchy as a function of getting older and doing a minimum level of work and then hitting the ceiling (12th grade) where you must then leave, your position in the hierarchy of work has to do with value to the company. The more valuable you are, the higher you climb. In school, you get pushed through the ranks (because you age as time passes). At work, one can rise or fall in positions based on what they do (or don't do) and even be ejected (fired) from the hierarchy altogether.

Voluntary/Involuntary

Perhaps the most challenging aspect for children to imagine about the work world is that it is, at its root, a voluntary activity. Child labor laws included putting limits on work for children and creating expectations for education. Each state in the US has its own set of rules about how long children must go to school. Most make formal schooling compulsory to about the age of 16. After the age of 16, children are ostensibly allowed to choose whether or not they want to go to school. Except in rare situations, society compels children to complete school by finishing the final grade (12th) or completing an equivalency exam. I say "compelled" because most know that people who do not have a diploma have trouble finding work that will earn them a living wage. Society makes necessary the act of achieving a diploma, even if it is not a formal law.

Work, on the other hand, is voluntary. No one must work. Most people choose to work, mainly because not-working is worse than working. Almost everyone who works until retirement age discovers this fact. People who have been fired, laid off, or had to take extended leave from work because of health issues almost unanimously report that not-working is worse than working, even if they also complain about having to work. Many retired people who see retirement as a reward for working a long time decide to do work of some sort.

What does this mean if you shift rapidly from an involuntary activity to a voluntary one? Most people who do not make the shift right away get fired. Since children are required (involuntarily) to go to school, the administration cannot fire them from school. Even if they are expelled from school (similar to firing), they must attend another school and some school must enroll them. On the contrary, if an employer fires a person, they can choose to leave the workforce. Additionally, if they choose to continue working, getting a new job can be significantly harder than the previous. Workplaces do not have to take you on as a worker.

Consider work completion. If a worker is not completing their work, what are the options of the workplace? Getting fired is often the outcome of failure to complete work or even substandard work completion. You can be removed, finally, from the workplace. What is the recourse if a person does not meet their work requirements and cannot be fired? This dilemma is what happens in school all the time. People in the top parts of the hierarchy (e.g., teachers) have to work harder to make sure people in the lower positions (e.g., students) do the activities they are supposed to do. A student can refuse to do work or indicate they are unable, and this does not necessarily make the student's job harder. It makes the teacher's job harder, and the teacher must work harder because they <u>can</u> get fired (they're operating under voluntary employment). Many people who move from the student role to the worker role do not have a good sense of who is responsible for applying effort. They also have a false belief about what the people above them in the hierarchy owe them.

The involuntary nature of school creates unique power dynamics within the hierarchy. Those dynamics change again when the person's presence becomes voluntary in the work setting. Unfortunately, schools do not sufficiently train many children to make this shift in their thinking and functioning.

Reward for Effort

If there were no benefits, we would not apply effort. There would not even be an expectation to apply effort if there were no apparent benefits to us. We do something to get something. There is an effort/reward exchange in school, but it looks much different from the exchange in the work world.

What do children in school get out of applying effort? Ultimately, children are given increased freedom for their effort. A primary goal of most students is eventually to finish being a student or to graduate from school. Children also apply effort to increase their grades which expands their options for other academics and careers. Broadened career aspirations connect us to things like relationships and commodities (cars, houses, etc.). In actuality, children apply effort in school to either get praise (which has actual value since people who are happy with you give you more stuff, including freedom) or get more choice (including being free from scrutiny). Freedom, independence, choice: these are all the direct outcomes from applying effort in school. Teachers absurdly use their own effort to demonstrate this link between effort and freedom in their students. When students are under-performing, teachers are often expected to spend more time correcting tests, giving feedback, re-teaching material, tutoring, and directing their students so they can continue on the progressive course toward freedom.

Interestingly, society grants freedom to most people as a function of getting older. What else is a function of getting older in school? It's moving up in the hierarchy. The reward system is absurd to the savvy but short-sighted pupils because they will get more freedom whether they apply maximum or minimal effort. Perhaps they will get more freedom sooner if they work harder, but freedom is inevitable. So schools developed a grading system to help children understand the exchange of effort for freedom. Indeed, if we assign value to something, even an arbitrary value, we can demonstrate that people will work for it. Just look at the dollar bill. It's paper, but people will apply a lot of effort to obtain it.

So, who benefits when the student and the teacher apply effort in school? The student. The focus is always on the student. Is the student getting sufficient support, quality instruction, and plenty of love and acceptance? Well, are they applying effort? If not, let's give them more resources so they will hopefully start trying harder. We want the student to succeed. The whole institution is geared toward student success. We even measure the effectiveness of schools based on student success. More often than not, research suggests this measurement process is unfair (e.g., urban school settings).

Who or what ultimately benefits from the effort of the worker? You can argue that the harder workers work, the more they get paid. But ultimately, the worker's work is supposed to benefit the workplace. If a worker's effort is not helping the business, the business replaces the worker or eliminates the position.

Workplaces try to figure out how to get the worker to work harder. This effort is generally not for the good of the worker but the interest of the business. Shifting from a context that is all about the student's good to one about the company's good is often a difficult adjustment for people first entering the workplace. In this sense, the school is the absolute wrong place to train people to work for any other benefit than their own since school is, at its core, about the student. When the student starts to work less, people at the top of the hierarchy are expected to work more. No workplace operates (or even can sustainably operate) like this.

It turns out that the home is a much better place to train a child for the workplace in this regard. I have had much more success making adjustments so that families, rather than schools, better resemble businesses. Schools are much too complex to make relevant changes. Teaching a child how their efforts benefit the whole (and thus, the individual child) is much easier to do in the family context. Running families more like businesses is seen as unloving or unsupportive and consequently unpopular in modern society. As a result, many families miss the chance to teach their children to be successful in the work world (to their detriment and the inadvertent increase of their children's dependence).

Basic Rules of the Work World

Most people have heard of the distinction between "soft skills" and "hard skills." Hard skills are those skills that are specific to your job. For example, if you work for a landscaper, hard skills can be knowing how to plant a tree or mow a lawn. On the other hand, soft skills are skills that apply to nearly every job. For instance, being on time to work is a soft skill. Society expects both landscapers and pediatricians to show up to work on time.

It just so happens that soft skills encompass most of the basic rules of the workplace. Here is a shortlist of some of the most prolific, standard, and heavily applied soft skills.

Punctuality

The 9 to 5 job means that work begins at 9 am and finishes at 5 pm. A person must be ready to work at 9 am (not pulling into the parking lot) and work until 5 pm (not packing their bag and getting ready to go home at 4:45 pm). Being late to work is one of the easiest ways to get fired. I do not think this is because, as a culture, we value being on time so much. We have the phrase "time is money," but I don't believe that applies here. The society holds punctuality in such high regard in the workplace because it is easy to measure. The expectation is very concrete (be ready to work by 9 am), there are potentially tons of raters (even children can tell the difference between 9 am and 9:01 am), and time is easily measured with a high level of precision (there are clocks all over the place). An event starting late or "going late" at work seems to create considerable stress in the work environment. The fewer bosses one has (i.e., if you're higher in the hierarchy), the more the group tolerates your lack of punctuality, but lack of timeliness is always counted against people. The other reason I think we count tardiness against people is that time is a fixed commodity. Once it's gone, it's gone.

In the same way, we look down on "knocking off early" (e.g., leaving work before 5 pm or the end of the day). This fact was something I learned on the job years ago. Because of the nature of my work, I had little to do for 5-10 minutes before quitting time. As a result, I started leaving when my work was done, which was before the end of the day. My boss warned me to fulfill my contract (stay until quitting time) or be replaced. Completing my work was not the issue. Fulfilling my contract and working until the end of the workday was the issue.

Polite and Formal

With some exceptions, the work environment is formal. There are standards for how to dress and behave. There are specific standards for how to speak. These standards are also in place in school, but the school tolerates and even expects constant pushback from students against these standards. That is the whole reason for the position of Vice-Principal in most schools. Pushback against the rules is generally considered developmentally appropriate for teenagers in modern society. No one effectively pushes against these formal standards in the workplace. Even if someone is annoyed by a standard, they rarely question it. Formal behavior is the expectation, and failure to apply to formality is another easy way to get removed from the system (fired).

How can the work world tolerate such formality for so long? After all, the work world is not necessarily evolving into a less formal environment. The formality must serve some purpose. The work world most likely became formal. Formality, for the most part, is a function of relationships. Even if some people in the workplace are friends (or even family members), the primary relationship (the "hat" they wear) while at work is "co-worker." Less frequently, it's employer/employee. A friend is never the primary relationship at work. Formality provides a common set of expectable standards that help maintain and support the co-worker and employer/employee relationship.

A final note about formality and politeness: some may argue that we are becoming less formal in the work setting. If you watch TV, you will find many examples of people being informal in the workplace and getting away with it. I want to be clear with the reader that these are stories, which means they are fiction. Being informal in the workplace is possible but extremely difficult and complicated. The cost of being unsuccessful is exceptionally high, so I do not recommend it to anyone wondering why some people can break the formality rule while others cannot. It is rarely an injustice and almost always a skill when someone breaks a formality rule. Do not mistake this statement for my belief in the absence of injustice in the workplace. However, if you cannot describe or appreciate the skill associated with breaking formality rules, you should never try to do it. Instead, formality rules are always appropriate in the workplace. You will never be disciplined, even if some criticize you for being too formal or polite.

Do your job

"Complete your work. Ask for help if you get stuck. Ask for more work if you finish early." It is a simple set of expectations that I teach people I counsel who are entering the work world or struggling to perform in the work world. This mantra is the same for the fry cook at a fast-food restaurant and the lawyer working on a big case.

Completing your work can sound very basic, but I cannot overstate the importance of doing more than a majority of a task. Also, letting or expecting others to do some of the jobs you were assigned is a very bad idea. Schools, unfortunately, do give partial credit, and parents helping with homework often fill in the blanks for some kids because they feel the child understands the information and don't want to belabor the task. Also, rush jobs are wrong, both at school and at work. The work world expects, in general, for the worker to apply 100% attention and effort to everything that is assigned. Every task is assigned because it needs someone to do it. Sloppy work is a problem because it makes the worker look bad and often makes the manager and the company look bad. Businesses will always trace messy and incomplete work back to the source: the worker.

Asking for help is hard for just about everyone in the workplace. Failure to ask for help usually comes from a fundamental misunderstanding about the relationship between the worker and the manager/supervisor. Most people do not know, and often those that know do not believe, that the manager's job is to make the worker successful. It is the manager's job because the manager is responsible for the worker's work and cannot possibly do both the worker's work and their own. So, the manager must focus on worker success which includes, primarily, competence in assignment completion. Asking for help is telling the manager: "help me be better at my job." Only foolish managers would ignore this or punish a worker for such a statement. If a worker gets penalized for asking for help, I recommend immediately looking for a new job. Unfortunately, there are bad managers out there. Usually, adequate managers appreciate appropriate requests for support. It is possible, however, to ask for help too much. This mistake also comes from both mismanagement (the company made a "bad hire") and misunderstanding of the role of the manager (they are there to make <u>you</u> do <u>your</u> job, not <u>do</u> your job).

The worker is at work to work, ultimately. If you finish a task early, that doesn't mean you no longer have a reason to be at work or can now relax or play at work. Managers expect you to ask for more work. You are at work to work. Some workplaces, especially those that offer salaried positions, can promote inaction at work. Workplaces never state that outright, but that becomes the mood of the workplace. In this case, I also recommend finding a new job. I worked, once, for a landscaper that was salaried. Usually, landscapers get paid hourly or by job, so there is an incentive to work harder (i.e., you make more money). The salaried landscaper had no incentive to work harder. His goal was to avoid getting fired by completing the minimum level of work. This landscaper and I drove around town in the truck when we finished a job early. He called them "hot laps." This job was terrible because it was boring and monotonous, and nothing I did that was not all about avoiding getting fired had any purpose. I love my current job because I have so much I could be doing, and all of it matters. Be the kind of worker that asks for more work when you complete all assigned tasks.

Respect the hierarchy

Like most of the rest of society, the work world is organized hierarchically. I mean that there are people up top and others down below. Geometrically, hierarchies often resemble a triangle pointing at the sky with a broad base. As one rises in the hierarchy, they have fewer peers (people on the same level). The most straightforward hierarchy in society is only two levels: parent and child. The British Monarchy is famous for having a highly complex hierarchy. Some businesses have very complicated hierarchies, and others have more simplistic hierarchies. Business hierarchies tend to become more complex as the business ages. Most companies will have a graph that describes their hierarchy. The pattern depicted can also be described as a "chain of command." Most people focus on the power and authority within the hierarchy, and for this reason, most people want to move up in the hierarchy. Most societies believe that having more authority is always better. The best way I have to describe the nature of a hierarchy in the work world is that people are responsible for everyone below them, and not the other way around. A manager is responsible for the workers, and the workers are never responsible for the manager. Responsibility always points downward, never up.

Why should you care?

Since there is a definable structure to the relational system in the workplace, you can guess how you should interact with almost anyone in the workplace if you are unsure. For instance, formality is the norm with people above and below you in the hierarchy. Polite behavior will always be appropriate, but people must use polite behavior with those above and below. If there is more casual behavior in the workplace, it will happen with peers or people on the same level. People moving up the hierarchy at different rates can create interpersonal discomfort. For instance, if a peer gets promoted above you, you might be expected to shift from casual to formal interaction rules. People above can punish people below, but it does not work in reverse. We can only punish those for whom we are responsible.

You cannot tell people above or beside you what to do. Delegation is only appropriate when you become formally elevated over someone or a group. This strict order is also why we call it "bossing someone around" when telling them what to do. Only bosses tell people (those below them) what to do.

People rarely move down in the hierarchy. This movement is called a demotion and is usually a punishment. More often, people get fired as opposed to getting demoted. Some people will choose to quit rather than be demoted. Our heavy societal emphasis on moving up the hierarchy makes some strategic moves down the hierarchy not even occur to people. People report feeling ashamed of demotion like it is a failure. Many autistic people I have worked with have sought demotions to work in a preferred position. Seeking a demotion is not the norm, but certain voluntary demotions can be highly beneficial to the individual and the company. Unfortunately, society places a heavy emphasis on promotion. This heavy emphasis has caused numerous problems in the work world. The most famous of these is called the "Peter Principle," where individuals are promoted based on their work competence to the point where they are finally incompetent and then stay in that position. Despite the absurdity of this practice, this seems to be how much of the work world continues to operate.

How to Break Rules

Years ago, when I was working in a high school for neurodiverse individuals, one Senior approached me with the task of "pulling a Senior Prank." This student had heard of other legendary Senior Pranks and had seen some on TV shows and wanted my help as the person with some administrative seniority and who also taught social skills classes to pull the ultimate Senior Prank. I let him know that I was not aware of anyone ever pulling such a prank at the school, which seemed to encourage rather than discourage him.

The tradition of Senior Prank is well established in American High School folklore. Seniors or those in the final year of their formal education (12th grade) coordinate a massive "prank" on the school. Traditionally such pranks are letting wildlife or farm animals into the school, placing desks and furniture on the school's roof, or the like. Sometimes the auto shop class will disassemble a teacher's car and reassemble it in the lunchroom. Such pranks are elaborate, thoughtful, or grand. Interestingly, these pranks are also rarely destructive or deadly. The point of the stunt is to be memorable and funny and not mean or hurtful.

I knew that this student trying to pull such a prank was not a good idea. The school was very formal, and the level of creativity and planning to pull off such a prank was beyond what I had seen in this student. I considered the task, and the more I thought about it, the more I realized that pulling this prank would be tricky, even with sufficient skills. The fundamental problem of the Senior Prank is that it is the active breaking of a rule that draws no punishment and, in most cases, garners praise. That was why the student wanted to do such a thing: he had heard tales of fantastic pranks pulled at other schools and wanted to add glory to his name for such a prank. How does a person add all recognition and no condemnation through the active breaking of a rule? And especially in a primarily fair system like a high school? I decided that the fundamental and necessary component of such an activity was a razor-sharp and deep understanding of the meaning and purpose of the rules the person is planning to break. I decided this student couldn't pull off such a prank because of a shallow and insufficient understanding of the rules.

And that is the key: to break the rules, one must fully and deeply understand the rules. Understanding is different, of course, from agreeing with the rules. People who fully understand rules can also respect and follow the rules while disagreeing entirely about the rules. I began to test this idea with dozens of other people I worked with who were on the spectrum over the years, and I found something interesting. While my clients and students on the spectrum were geniuses at following the rules, most of them had a very shallow understanding of the purpose of individual regulations. I would ask questions such as "how did they make up this rule" or "why does this rule make sense?" How does this rule keep people safe or contribute to the common good? Most of the people I talked to would ultimately reason that the rule didn't make sense or that they could come up with a superior rule if only people would listen to them. They felt that the people in charge made rules up randomly or impulsively or that people in charge did lots of things without sufficient reason. They also believed it was customary to follow an absurd rule and that much of life was similarly disorganized and confusing.

The people you see breaking the rules and being admired for violating rules have a profound understanding of and respect for rules. A classic example of this is professional comedians. The more a comedian "breaks the rules," the more people like them. Conventional comedians don't last long. Comedians are primarily skilled at observation and understanding systems, including how and why they work, and it is this skill, among others, that makes them competent comedians.

Recall I said earlier in this chapter that if you don't understand how or why a person was able to break the rules and get away with such behavior, you should not try to break the rules. Did you know that teasing is a good example of both the good and bad effects of breaking rules? Teasing can both hurt a person's feelings and build a person's self-esteem. Do you know why this is? If you don't, never tease someone. Until you understand how teasing can both tear down and build up, you should never tease someone due to the potentially destructive nature of the behavior. I assure you that this effect of teasing is not random to both build and destroy.

At work, I generally recommend people do not actively break the rules. However, most people comment to me that some people at work break rules and don't seem to get in trouble for it. Is this injustice? Possibly, but not necessarily. This person likely has a deep understanding of the rules they are breaking and can break them so that they avoid criticism or even gain appreciation.

Chapter 2

Toward a Career

Just about every science fiction story set in the future deals directly or indirectly with the issue of work. Utopian settings view work as a thing of the past or something one does because they enjoy and get meaning out of it, and certainly not as a way to survive. Dystopian stories picture work as a punishment or something forced on people at the lower end of society. Both of these extremes view work as an accessory – it's something with which to punish (dystopian) or reward (utopian) people. However, work and our need to work seem to be something much more ingrained in us. People seem to need to work to be healthy. Interestingly, work can also be a significant source of stress, both physically and emotionally. Like everything in our lives, the things we need to survive can kill us in varying amounts and under certain situations.

Why do we work?

In the US, people generally start working full time by their early 20s and plan to stop working in their late 60s. Most people work full time for 40-50 years of their lives. Practically speaking, most people work eight hours a day, five days a week, for 50 weeks a year. This schedule translates to 100,000 hours of work in typical adult life. Work consumes more than half of our waking hours for more than half of our lives. I imagine the only other activity we do that takes up more time is sleep. To that end, it would be essential to examine some reasons we work.

Participation in Society

Work is the primary way we demonstrate our value to society. Showing one's value is critical if we want society to continue to keep us in it. Even today, people fare best in groups, and to be part of most groups, you have to demonstrate your value to the group. In modern society, we do that primarily with money. And we get our money, mostly, from working. We show humanity that we are valuable and worth keeping around, and society gives us money that we use to participate in society and get our needs met by society. We provide a good or service, people pay us money for that good or service, and then we use that money to buy goods and services from others in society. If a person walks into a store and asks for a candy bar for free because they don't have money, the store will ask them to leave. However, if that same person walks into the same store and offers enough money for that same candy bar, the clerk will sell them the candy bar. The only difference is the money. Money is a ticket for participation. If you don't think this is the case, ask a poor person how easy it is to participate in society. It is nearly impossible to achieve fundamental participation in society without money, such as shelter, healthcare, or food. And this includes communities that have way more of these things than they could ever use. In most cases, society would rather throw something away than give it to someone for free. This demonstrates to me that we work to earn money to participate in society.

Income

Practically speaking, money pays for everything. Everything in society can be monetized. Of the things necessary for daily subsistence, only air seems to be free. I assure you that air is free only because people have not yet found a convenient way of selling it. Most people get most of their money through working.

Interestingly, we can figure out how much it costs to stop working. Retirement calculators will get some basic information about you, most notably your age, and estimate how much money you will need to have before retiring. So, money can even buy you a pass out of working.

Keeping busy and sharp

Working gives us something to do. There are groups of people who do not work. They are retired people, students on summer break, and people who are unemployed because they were fired or laid off. Generally speaking, after a certain amount of time, people in these groups gravitate toward one type of activity: entertainment. Your brain needs stimulation, and the days when you are not working seem to become longer and longer. If you are a young adult who has been out of work for more than a month, ask yourself what your primary engagement is during your waking hours. Most people I talk to say they spend most of their hours being entertained or seeking out entertainment. One of the reasons for this is that our brains crave input and abhor unabated boredom. We look to TV, videos, video games, and the like for such stimulation. People often report that the excitement of the game or TV show has worn off, and mostly they watch or play to keep the boredom away. Work saves us from this. Most people on vacation look forward to returning to their job (if they genuinely enjoy it). Many retirees end up doing some sort of work after being retired. Laid-off workers usually find looking for a job more challenging, while they want more and more to get employed.

Working helps to keep people mentally sharp and socially connected. Some jobs are monotonous, but most work has something in it that is engaging. If the actual work itself is not attractive, social interactions in the job are interesting. Work helps keep us "in the loop." Most jobs require interaction with groups of people who then connect us with other parts of society. These connections and interactions create networks of people. Most people work, and work itself has a routine shared by most workers. For instance, most people go to work in the morning and come home in the late afternoon after about eight hours of work. Most people take two days off each week, on the weekend, so most people also have free time at the same time. No one invites me to go to the beach on a Tuesday at 10 am because they assume (correctly) that I am at work. On the other hand, they will text me Tuesday at 10 am and ask me to go to the beach on Saturday at 10 am. I will almost always say yes because I rarely work on Saturday morning, and I love the beach.

Meaning and Purpose

Now we are getting into the need or *drive* to work. I remember a concept from my early training called the "terminal drop." Research demonstrates that many people die in the first five years of retirement. Many variables explain this finding, but one that stuck out to me is that people retire, get bored, and then die. As much as people can complain about working, and there is a lot to complain about, work can give our lives meaning and purpose. Without purpose, it is hard to live. Work gives us something to do that matters if we do it or not. It provides us with a place to be at a specific time and people who care whether or not we are there. Work gives us the opportunity to be rewarded for what we do and how we do it. That constant feedback of "it matters that you're here," "here's how much we appreciate what you are doing," "your effort and opinion matters," and all of the other messages we get from working are important to us. We need such feedback not only to straighten us out but also to encourage us. My most vigorous complaints about jobs have not been about the work, but that my work didn't matter. Even now, I would rather scrub a toilet than do something that nobody knows or cares about or that benefits nobody.

Need one to get one

On a practical note, it's harder to get a job if you are out of work than if you're gainfully employed. Said another way, the time to look for a new job is while you have one. People report that this advice is confusing to them, so allow me to explain. Potential employers are trying to figure out if you will be a good employee. Having a job makes you look like a better employee than if you are out of work. People can be out of work for many reasons, but one of those is that they are terrible employees. Being employed implies you are probably a good employee. So, if a potential employer is looking at several qualified applicants and needs to choose between them, those who are currently unemployed will be passed over. It's an easy choice to make from the perspective of an employer. To get the job you want, you should be employed. The first thing the potential employer looks at is your resume, and it is best if your resume lists you are currently successfully employed.

If you are currently employed, you may ask why you would be looking for a job? I will address this question later, but the short answer is that no job is perfect. However, good workers are constantly looking for an increasingly ideal positions.

Socializing

All people need to socialize to be healthy. Isolation is not suitable for humans, even those who say they prefer it. I have not met a healthy, isolated person. Solitary confinement was recently deemed a "cruel and unusual punishment" for incarcerated people. There are limits to how long a person can spend in solitary confinement, regardless of their crime, because extended isolation is torture to people. I bring this up to highlight the argument I get from many people who say they choose isolation because it makes them feel better. I have never seen this be the case. Isolation may solve some problems, but it creates a host of other, more devastating problems.

We all need socializing, and work offers most adults the best option for regular, healthy doses of socializing. Most adults I know also make most of their friends through work. Indeed, many people come home from socializing at work all day and want to socialize more. The people they invite to socialize outside of work are usually co-workers. Work provides people chances to socialize and is a great option for a social life.

The largest, most significant body of work that most people achieve occurs at work. We can indeed look at individual achievements and find those in people that are significant and happened outside of work. For instance, I wrote my first book in the evenings between getting home from work and putting my child to bed. I chipped away at the book for an hour a day for months, and it was a considerable achievement to get that book published. That book, however, is nothing compared to the body of work I will achieve going to work for 100,000 hours over 50 years. The power of work to produce achievement is in its regularity and routines. Some days are meaningful, but overall more gets done on the average days. These are the days when I would prefer to stay home in bed instead of going to work. I get out of bed and into the car because people expect me to be there and get stuff done. As a result, I do get things done. People who want to impact the world or be remembered for anything should get a job and work it day in and day out.

In this section, I have done my best to choose what I think are more universal reasons to work. Everyone who works will benefit on some level from the issues listed above. Included are so-called "homemakers," or adults who primarily do the job of raising children and managing a household. I have left out a host of other good reasons to work that are personal to me. For instance, I like my job. Going to work means I get to do something I like. I would probably choose to spend more time working if I did not have other obligations. I know that not everyone enjoys what they do, but many people do. And being able to like your job is an excellent reason to keep working, developing experience, getting educated, building your resume, and creating a network of people to move closer and closer to the job you love. I haven't done an official count, but my current job might be my 20th. I just kept working, and when the opportunity presented itself, I moved into a better job. And here I am.

How to Get Hired

Many people reading this book may have a poor work history. Included in that group are people who have no work history. The work world has created a Catch-22 for new workers in that most desirable jobs require experience. Who are the people with experience, and how are they getting experience? Essential for the worker who wants a job, or a better job, is to figure out what the employer is seeking. If you have been working for a while, use these items to check your fitness as a worker. So, here are the Top 10 reasons you will get hired for the job you want.

10. You have a resume.

It is still surprising how many people contract with me to help them get and be successful in a job and do not have a resume. Even stranger are the people who refuse or avoid, for whatever reason, creating a resume for themselves. Some resumes are better than others, but a terrible resume is better than no resume. Another truth is that your resume will and should get better the longer you work, but to make your resume better, you actually need to work. Many people try to solve the problem of a bad resume before they start working. It is incredibly challenging to improve your resume without working. It is a better use of your time to get the job you can with the resume you have and then work on improving your resume, than to try to improve your resume to get the job you want.

9. You primarily pursue jobs for which you are qualified.

I have talked with many college graduates with no work experience who are frustrated that they cannot find work in their field. Research highlights part-time work experience in high school as a predictor for vocational success after college. Having no work experience disqualifies you for many jobs, even those in your field of study. Previously we talked about the differences between the work world and the educational world. These differences are fundamental to employers. A person can indeed learn a complex skill without learning any soft skills, and employers want soft skills. If all you have is the educational requirements for a job, you are missing about 50% of the total requirements.

All of this is to say that if you have a degree in nuclear engineering with no previous work experience, the job you might be most qualified for is working as a janitor at a nuclear power plant. Aim for the job you are eligible for primarily. Of those suitable jobs, aim for the one you want.

8. You have adequate communication skills.

A person needs to be able to both talk and write about their skills and goals as a worker. The importance of writing is not just true for people who want to be writers but also for those who went into a field, like engineering, to avoid writing (and speaking with humans). There is simply no way to avoid communicating with people if you are looking for a job. A person looking for work should practice talking about what they can and want to do and write about those things as well. What about people who have a "communication disorder" like autism? The work world is trying to adjust hiring expectations to attract neuro-diverse people, and I think this is reasonable and even mutually beneficial. However, I have not seen anyone eliminate the need for communication in the hiring process. Also, I have not seen anyone successfully eliminate the need to communicate within a job. Good communication increases efficiency and productivity. I've already made the case that socializing at work is healthy. Even if communication is a problem for you, you can improve your communication skills. Indeed everyone can improve their communication skills.

7. You apply for jobs.

There seem to be many theories about the best ways a person can get their dream job, but ultimately the one that wins out is that which supports applying for many jobs. Sometimes unemployment is low, and sometimes it's high. Sometimes employers are hiring, and sometimes not. Some fields have lots of employment, and some have few. Regardless of the job market, you have to apply to many jobs if you want a job. People can generate lots of reasons not to apply for jobs. Some tell me that no one is hiring. I also hear that there are no jobs they want, no jobs they feel qualified for, or no jobs available where they want to work. None of these arguments are helpful if you're going to get hired at a job. Even people who have work may apply for jobs to see if their current job is still the best. Putting it this way may sound simplistic, but you get hired because you apply for jobs.

6. You have others look at your application.

It is essential to have other people look at and evaluate your job application. People should be looking at your resume and cover letter for coherence, grammar, and anything else that would disqualify you for consideration for a job. This process includes a job at the city's most prestigious law firm or a job at a fast-food restaurant. Many people disqualify themselves for employment through spelling errors on their resumes. Some people leave blanks on an application. If the job is worth having, others will likely also apply for that job. You should assume that that person had someone look at their application. I have evaluated applications on several occasions, and low-quality applications were one of the easiest ways to weed out applicants. Make your application look like you want the job, even if you don't. It is better to be offered the job and turn it down than never offered it.

On a personal note, I have applied for several teaching jobs that require me to lecture an actual class. This requirement makes sense since the "job test," or having people do the job they are applying for as part of the application process, is one of the most predictive elements of any job interview. My credentials, resume, cover letter, and references were good enough to get me a job test as a guest lecturer. I prepared and gave a brand new lecture since the topic given to me was one I had never lectured on before. Rather than test out my talk with an audience (it would have been straightforward since I was in grad school and surrounded by many other grad students in my field, also applying for jobs), I went in cold. I completely bombed the interview based on the lecture. There were less than adequate aspects of the lecture that could have been easily pointed out and changed if I had just given it to someone else for critique.

5. You are punctual.

As stated elsewhere, employers are very interested in soft skills, and punctuality is one of the primary soft skills. Being punctual means that you meet application deadlines. If you miss a deadline for the application, you most likely will not get the job regardless of how qualified you are. If you are late for an in-person interview or interview by phone, consider the interview over. Employers know that you are on your best behavior when applying for a job, so they know that people who are late for interviews will be late for important meetings, work deadlines, and mundane and rainy Wednesday mornings. They know they are saving themselves a lot of trouble by hiring someone who can at least get the basic expectations right in the interview process.

4. You have training.

Someone once told me she wanted to work as an "idea person." This person also told me she did not want to go through the hassle of getting a degree in the relevant field. She stated companies would hire her for this job because she had good ideas, and the lack of a suitable skill set would be unimportant. The reality is that the people who will become your bosses and co-workers if you get hired are people with degrees, and you have just told these people you think their degree is meaningless or not worth your time.

Everyone complains about all the things they "had" to learn that were unrelated to their primary interest or passion. Psychology is one of the primary classes people complain about to me, a psychologist. Let me state this bluntly: no one will take your word for it that you can do a job. They want proof. The degree or certificate from a respected institution of higher learning is your proof. Complain about what you had to do to get that "piece of paper," but the institution's reputation backs that piece of paper. Employers don't have to trust you because they trust the institution vouching for you.

Let's put this another way: adequate training includes both specific and general information, organized in a meaningful way by an expert. A composer I knew once said he had to master the conventional, fundamental way of doing things before he could improvise. Every discipline has a standard way to perform the profession, and you will get that job because you learned that conventional way. You have training.

3. You are flexible.

There is no perfect job. Even the job you think is the perfect job is not perfect. What you are looking for is the best job you can reasonably get. You have looked at specific needs for a job, such as level of pay or location, and you have prioritized those needs, but ultimately you want to work above all else. You understand that a person often must work their way into a job they love. To get the job you love, you are willing to work hard in a job you do not like.

There was a time I was preparing to finish grad school and looking for work. I went through the whole process of job hunting, enhancing my application, practicing the job interview, and the like. Unfortunately, the job market for what I was looking for was not great, and the time had come to start applying for jobs outside my discipline (e.g., barista). I was all set with driving to Starbucks for a latte and an application when I got a call from Dr. Stewart, the person that decided to take a chance on a new graduate. (Side note: I asked her once why she hired me, considering my application was not very strong. The job I applied for at Orion Academy was attractive but was low on my application list because I was not very qualified. Dr. Stewart confirmed that she initially hired me because I was male and one of the few male psychologists with basic level qualifications who applied. So there you have it.)

2. You have experience.

You have had other jobs from which you were not fired. You have formal volunteer experience. You have worked in an internship and have formal work training. You also have people who have overseen your work willing to vouch for you. Under their oversight, you worked hard, did your best in the job, and did so with a consistently good attitude. When a potential employer calls your references, the reference says they would hire you back if you wanted to come back. So, not only have you worked in the past, you have people affirming that you did good work. It doesn't matter if you worked for a Fortune 500 company or a lawnmowing company. The point is that you did well in all your work. You did a good job, whatever the job was.

1. You are committed to working.

One of the most significant barriers to getting a job is the belief that it doesn't matter if you work. If you are struggling to find work, or a better position, ask yourself how essential it is for you to work. Some people ask this of themselves and discover that if they never worked again in their lives, they would do ok. They wouldn't be living in luxury, but they would at least be able to meet all of their essential needs. Many people in this situation have family who will care for them or receive government assistance. In these cases, the unemployed individual will do well to see employment and work as necessary for a good life, even if they can survive without work. In another scenario, ask yourself if you won the lottery and money was no longer an issue if you would stop working altogether. Some people say they would quit their job, but many say they would work less or get a dream job. Working is good for a person, and not-working is not good. Until the worker has this epiphany that "work is good," they will be less hungry to do a good job. Said another way, a person's disdain for work could be keeping them from getting a good job.

Getting a job is hard work. Keeping a job is hard work. If you are not committed to that hard work, you will not give it what it requires. This lack of urgency and necessity of working can result in missed interviews, low-quality applications, and dated or missing training and experience. The opinion that work, in general, is a prison or oppressive keeps you from getting all you can out of work. The longer a person is unemployed, the harder it will be to get a job. It is easy to let a week go by - and then a whole month - before getting on the computer to check the job listings. In that time, your application grows less and less appealing to an employer. Those committed to working and getting a job, or a better job as soon as possible, get hired.

Not Getting Hired

Here are the top 10 things that will get your application passed over, keep you from getting a job, or otherwise disqualify you from working.

10. Low-quality application

Consider typos, incomplete, and bad grammar. I have seen applications with the wrong potential employer listed, some with foul language and the like. In traditional hiring situations, the application, specifically the resume, is the most predictive of success as an employee for that company. Employers know that what applicants list on the application is your absolute best work and your best try at formal, professional language.

9. Not checking email

Email has become a primary means of professional communication. To that end, many people I work with who are job hunting report they do not check email or have a professional email. As a result, they miss essential communications from potential employers. While they ignore their emails, others respond and get the job. I recommend that all adults, especially job seekers, check their email daily. Job seekers should probably check it more often. You should also have an email address that doesn't make you sound ridiculous.

8. Slow turnaround

Employers want to know you're eager for the job. Someone will be keen on the job, and that's the one that will get the job. Eager people return messages right away. Also, most companies have a policy about turnaround time on messages that you may be inadvertently violating (even before being hired) by sitting on a message too long.

7. You sound strange.

The initial real-time contact with a potential employer is vital. If you answer your phone sounding angry, tired, drunk, confused, or in any other off-putting way, you will not get the job. Practice being cheerful on the phone or during an interview. Practice answering the phone in an "approachable" way. I was always amazed at the tough-guy way people answered the phone on TV shows (e.g., "Yeah?" "What?" "Go!"). Don't be like this. I remember my friend answering with a quick, cheerful greeting, and I adopted it right away: Hello, this is Andrew.

6. You are informal in the interview.

I used to think mock interviews were somewhat a waste of time until a young man entered my "office" to start the interview and immediately put his feet on my desk. Failure to understand and follow the basic expectations of formality in an interview or any work situation will make it hard to get the job. Also, I learned early on that if you have lunch during an interview, do not order soup. Too messy.

5. You don't want to work.

I cannot overstate how much your attitude is apparent to the people around you. People can see your lousy attitude right away and want nothing to do with it. Managers will not want to hire you; co-workers don't want to work with you. Therefore, cultivate a positive work attitude.

4. It's a long shot.

You should pursue your dream job, but you should not expect to get it. Why should you pursue it then? Because you might get it, and if you don't apply, you definitely won't get it. Still, don't expect to get it. I am bringing this up because many people apply for a longshot job, meaning there is very little chance they will get the job, and then when they don't get the job, they are devastated and find it hard to persist. So apply for the longshot job but don't expect to get it because it is a longshot.

3. You give up.

Don't give up. The universe is not going to have pity on you and send you a job. I bring this up because a line of reasoning out there says something like, "as soon as you stop trying so hard, you'll get your heart's desire." We apply this to relationships, jobs, the lottery, and any situation where we are subject to disappointment. In investigating this reasoning, I have found that people see the universe as not so much unfair or dispassionate, but cruel. They say I don't have something I want because the universe doesn't want me to be happy. So, if I stop desiring it, I'll be more likely to get it. This reasoning is seriously flawed, so be very careful about applying that reasoning to getting a job. You will get a job through hard work and persistence. And yes, there will be disappointment along the way.

2. You think the world owes you.

This reason is another attitude piece. I talk to many people who think they are doing the company a favor by applying for this position. This attitude influences every level of the application process and provides plenty of opportunities to reject your application. Some believe they are exceptional, and the company should acknowledge that. You are not unique, at least not in that way. You are special to your mother, but not to a business. They want someone to do a job, plain and simple.

1. You have no idea how to get a job.

Formative educational settings have been teaching "job skills" for a long time, but I am still amazed at how little people know about the hiring process who have not already been through it several times. To remedy this, teenagers should get part-time jobs. Experience is the best instructor in this case. It helps to go through the process from beginning to end with little to no expectations of getting a job. Parents who support their teens getting jobs report that the process is very complicated, even if individual steps are simplistic. Later in this chapter, we'll discuss the basics of the job application process.

The basics of how to get a job

For many people, getting a job, or getting a better job, is a mystery. It is a mystery, even for those who currently have a job because it is a relatively complex task that one rarely does. Current estimates are that people change jobs every 4-5 years. People retiring now say they have had about 12 jobs in their lifetime. To give you some perspective, I change the oil in my car every three months, my furnace filter every six months, and file my taxes yearly. I renew my psychologist license every two years. I can't think of anything critical that I routinely do less frequently than two years. I drain my hot water tank yearly and have to look up how to do it every time. Even though 12 jobs over a lifetime sounds like a lot, applying for a job at that rate is a very low-frequency activity. It makes sense that people don't recall all the steps and don't think about it all that often. After all, I hire someone to do my taxes because it is an infrequent and complicated activity with high stakes (i.e., pay a fine or go to jail if you do it wrong).

To apply for a job, one must work out many logistics, engage in planning, and carefully consider the job application process. Here are some of the tasks one must complete before they fill out their first job application

- Decide the kind of job they want
- Figure out how much they want to work and make (i.e., salary or pay)
- Figure out when they will be able to engage in the job application process (this is important because applying for jobs, attending interviews, and following up all take time. If you are applying for multiple positions, the amount of time to do all this is significant)
- Update/create a resume
- Track down former employers and gather letters of recommendation
- Write a cover letter
- Figure out how to keep track of the process (e.g., use a spreadsheet)
- Decide how you will get to and from the job
- Look at job openings

This list of activities could be shorter or longer based on your situation. The point is that getting a job is not usually something done on the spur of the moment. The process takes some planning and intentionality.

Several people have reported creating a routine out of applying for work. However, rather than engaging in the activity every 4 to 5 years, they tell me they do it annually. For instance, one academic administrator I talked to said he would apply to at least one job opening every summer. First, he would update his resume, make sure his references were up to date, and then find a job that sounded interesting to him. It is important to note that he did not do this because he hated his job. On the contrary, it was quite the opposite. He stated that he used the activity to make sure his work skills were up to date and that he was meeting the basic standards of his profession, among other things. He also stated that the activity often left him with increased confidence that his job was a good one and ideas about how to make it better.

Application

Once the preparation is complete, now you must apply for jobs. Some jobs have a formal, standard application, and others have a list of documents required for completing an application. It used to be the case that McDonald's had a giant tablet of blank applications. When someone was looking for a job, they would come into the store (or go through the drive-through) and request an application. The tablet was under the counter, and the manager would tear one-off and offer a pen so the applicant could sit in a booth and complete the application. The last time I applied for a university position, they needed a copy of my Curriculum Vitae (CV, an educator's version of a resume), three letters of recommendation, and a cover letter introducing myself. Sometimes copies of my scholarly work are requested.

The point is that the application process is very formal and standardized for most jobs. The application process must be completed fully and by the directions, or you should not expect to get hired for that job. Many people completing an application at McDonalds tell me they intended to complete it in the store but took it home because they didn't have a required piece of information memorized, like a Social Security Number or a pen. Plan for the completion and submission of applications to take some time. Do your absolute best work at all times.

The Waiting

Some jobs are looking for someone to work for them right away, and some have an application window with a deadline. Some positions get filled long after the application window closes. What happens to your application after submitting it is something of a mystery.

You should expect to see a description of the hiring process. For instance, an application deadline means that employers will not decide about the job until sometime after the deadline. Some jobs will post a start date, suggesting they will decide by that time. Why is this information helpful? Most people who want a job or a better job want one now. It is hard to know when waiting to hear about the bureaucratic progress is considered patience (i.e., you have to let things play out) or foolishness (i.e., you may be waiting to hear from one application before you pursue another).

I have noticed more job postings stating they do not want you to follow up on your application. It used to be the case, and perhaps it still is, that it was appropriate to follow up on your application once you submitted it. I recommend people follow up between one and two weeks of the application. This follow-up would come in an email to confirm they received your application and if there were "any other questions" about the application. This activity can show tenacity and intentionality and is another chance to demonstrate soft skills like formal and polite communication and the use of email. However, this activity can also be seen as being pushy and unnecessary. The follow-ups likely create a significant amount of work for the person receiving the application. Thus, some businesses are asking applicants not to follow up. During the waiting time, a person should track the stage of their application, when they should expect to hear, and any follow-up they have done or plan to do.

The Initial Response

Yes, No, and We Need More Information. These are the three responses you will get.

A "More Information" response is acceptable because it is not a "No" response. It means there is something about your application the company liked. This response is one reason you check email daily and even several times a day. Turning this response around and quickly providing the requested information is likely a big determiner of whether or not you will get hired. Remember that the company is likely "on the fence" about you-they can neither accept nor reject your application, and your response will help them make that decision.

A "No" response is unfortunate but usually requires at least one more activity from you. First, if possible, you should thank the company for something. In most cases, thank them for looking at your application. Why would you not just ignore it and move on or send them a "you don't know what you're missing" email? This situation becomes an opportunity to respond professionally to a company. After all, this is business and not personal, so respond in a business-like way. Second, you should always avoid burning bridges whenever you can. Why shut a door when there's no cost to leaving it open. If they don't hire you now, perhaps they will hire you in the future. After all, you will likely be looking for another job in five years.

A "Yes" response is excellent but not the end of the road. Remember, most of the time there are still a lot of decisions to be made. In some cases, you will be one of several people that compose a smaller group of applicants for one job. In other cases, there is still compensation and position to discuss. In addition, you may receive more than one job offer since you are likely applying for multiple jobs, and you will have to make an informed decision between good things. Finally, the company has still invested very little in you, and it would be easy for them to withdraw the offer of a job based on what you do next. The point is that you should reply right away and follow the next set of instructions from the company.

A verbal offer of a job is just that: an offer. It's not a job. At the very least, you have to go to the store, sign an employment contract and pick up your uniform. Many jobs have an in-person interview or even multiple interviews. Some have "job tests" where potential employers evaluate your ability to do the work described in the job posting. Some say you have the job "as long as your references check out." Once they know you're interested in the position, the company will do at least an additional round of reviewing your credentials, abilities, and skills. People practice for interviews, practice job tests (i.e., giving a lecture), and make sure they have formal clothing appropriate for the job. The point is that a positive response to your application ushers you not into a career but another set of tasks that will likely determine the fate of your employment. At this time, the company will give you more specific instructions, and again, you have the chance to demonstrate your skills or royally screw up your options. When I talked about the mock interview above where the student put his feet on my desk, this was the stage of the process where he screwed up. Feet on a desk meant an instant end to the process.

Closing the Process

Choosing one thing means not choosing an infinite number of items. If you buy a Snickers, you are not purchasing a Twix, Skittles, or Milky Way. Even if you only have one job offer and choose it, you will either stop looking for jobs or significantly reduce the amount of energy you are putting into the job search. You are, after all, now employed.

The job search process must change at some point, especially if you get a job. Traditionally, people imagine they will stop looking for work. However, realistically, the job search process is ongoing in activities like updating one's resume, updating one's skills, checking job postings, and about once every five years (on average), starting the whole process over.

Isn't it just a piece of paper?

There are a couple of questions I get from almost everyone with whom I work on the topic of getting a job and building it into a career. The first is, "What's the big deal with getting a degree anyway?" Most of the people I work with had a hard time in school. Once they complete high school, going to school for another four to 10 years is abhorrent to most. Even if they did well academically, they struggled socially. Some struggled on every level, and most never understood why they had to work so hard at something so seemingly pointless and challenging.

"It's just a piece of paper" makes a lot of sense when you look at what it takes for some people to get it. But I want to caution the reader that it is not just a piece of paper. The degree or diploma is described better as a voucher. A voucher is an object that represents something earned or deserved, and it is backed up by someone with a good and solid reputation. The more substantial the person's reputation is backing you up, the more valuable, reliable, and meaningful the voucher is.

Why do you need a voucher to get a job? When a company hires you, they are guessing what kind of worker you will be. Namely, they hope that you will be a good worker. A good worker works hard and can either do or learn how to do the job. And, after they hire you for a job, they will spend considerable resources training you to work within the company's structure. Most companies have three months following your hire where they make sure you are a good fit for the job. In this Probationary Period, they spend a lot of time and money training you, but will withhold some of your pay (usually in the form of health insurance) and job security (i.e., they can fire you without warning or explanation).

Why won't they just take your word that you can do the job? The primary reason is that you have a motive to lie. I am not saying that you will lie, just that if you did lie about your qualifications and abilities, it would make a lot of sense (but still be wrong). In most cases, a person must work for a while for the company to recuperate the costs of hiring and training you. They are taking a risk with all new employees, and they want to reduce the risk as much as possible. One of the main ways to reduce that risk is by requiring a "piece of paper" for all applicants.

It can be easy for those who do not have a degree or diploma to underestimate how hard it is to get one. If it weren't hard to get a legitimate degree, there would be no industry offering cheap and fast diplomas (there is) or fraudulent degrees (there are). Even the primary college degree, called the Bachelor's Degree, requires at least four years of intensive, full-time work, usually at considerable expense. In addition, people will incur massive debt for one of these degrees. So beware that the piece of paper you scorn was very costly to the people who have one, and to them, it represents the basic level of assurance that you can do a job. Without one, you are unqualified for most jobs you want to work. Additionally, I want to stress that this exclusion is not unfair or unjust. People learn things and gain useful experience while working to obtain one of these pieces of paper.

I'm the best person for the job, so why didn't they hire me?

There are a couple of things going on here. The first has to do with our old friend, Theory of Mind. Even though you know you are highly qualified, passionate, and dedicated, there is a lot that you think or know about your fitness for the job that other people do not. You have to tell them directly for them to know. Also, it is not necessarily their job to tease that information out of you, but yours to give to them. There are usually multiple applicants for one position, or more applicants than positions, so it's the applicant who must do more of the selling. Sometimes you will note the reverse: there is a job listed that no one wants. In this case, the company will do the wooing. Recently I saw a posting that offered a $500 bonus to new hires. This offer means the company has a hard time finding qualified applicants. This offer may also mean no one wants to do the job. So being wooed by a job you want is kind of rare. You should expect to have to do the wooing initially.

The second issue has to do with the Good Enough Principle. More often than not, it is not realistic to do one's absolute best. I understand that this flies in the face of everything you were taught in school, but it is true. More often, the best thing to do is good enough. One chooses a good enough burrito from the menu, and the burrito maker makes it good enough to meet your expectations. I mow my lawn until it is good enough. Most of my parenting is good enough. Much of this book will be composed of good enough explanations of concepts and terms. Most jobs say they are looking for the best of the best workers out there. Mostly, they are looking for a good enough employee. They must confirm the applicant is qualified and low risk. Surveying seven billion people every time you have an opening on your fry cook line is not a good use of resources. The Good Enough Principle probably also explains why you had both excellent and average teachers. This is why your parents made mistakes. We not only aim for good enough in most of our efforts, but we also tolerate it in others. This tolerance exists despite society telling people always to do their best. So, another reason they didn't hire you, the best person for the job, is that they weren't looking for the best; they were looking for someone good enough.

On a personal note, I want to say that there were likely always better applicants for positions in which I was eventually hired. There was always someone better, and I am grateful for the good enough policy because it gave me a chance to prove myself. These good enough decisions are an opportunity to exceed expectations, so hopefully, someone will see you as good enough someday and set up a chance for you to exceed expectations in your work.

People must be faithful and competent with little things before managers put them in charge of bigger things. It is true that being "thrown into the deep end" can be a defining moment for some people, but this activity is rarely a matter of course. In most cases, one works their way to better jobs. You will see evidence of this principle everywhere in the work world. For instance, CEOs are still judged based on their punctuality, and entry-level jobs are a whole category of work. Working your way up and "pulling yourself up by your bootstraps" are descriptions of this concept and are seen as universally virtuous processes. One answer to the question above is that this is how the world works. The method of working one's way up defines the work world.

Does it have to work that way, though? Yes. As mentioned above, most of what I do all day, and especially those things for which I am judged most successfully, are soft skills. See my note about people considering the punctuality of CEOs. Even though they do not usually get fired for being late, workers will complain about CEOs starting meetings late or not ending on time. Soft skills are often the focus of entry-level jobs that employees must master before moving to a higher-level position. A person in a higher-level job cannot usually afford to focus on soft skill development because the job requires more hard skill activity. The job also tends to have a more significant impact on others and the company. Therefore, your mistakes in a higher-level position can harm a more substantial number of people and processes. Errors based on soft skills are problematic because people expect you to know and have mastered soft skills. Some people in authority actively break soft skill rules to exert their seniority and separateness from the group. You can only do this if the standard is soft skill compliance.

In summary, much of the work world structure is based on the notion of working one's way up. But, of course, this is not a new convention. On the contrary, workers have been starting at the bottom and working their way up for millennia.

If we all work for the company's benefit, why does it feel like I compete with my co-workers?

Competition is one of the best ways to get people to do more than the minimum. Some people are indeed more competitive than others, but making specific resources more scarce so that people will work harder to achieve them is again a foundational principle of our society. Competition is one of the main ways the workplace pushes its workers to do more than "good enough" work. Now that you have seen the method, are you exempt from its influence? Probably not. Many things the company offers as a reward for "winning" at work are desirable. Interestingly, research finds that the impact of the primary motivator, money, tends to plateau at a very predictable point. For example, in 2010, it was around $75,000. After this point, people seem to need other things, like increased status, more flexible work hours, or more exciting work to motivate them to compete and bring their A-Game.

Getting fired

Don't get fired. Getting fired is not the end of the world, but it does make life harder. Recently I was talking to someone who was delaying getting their passport renewed. They couldn't find a convenient time to do it and didn't have any planned trips. Finally, they were thinking about traveling again and sat at the computer and discovered that the grace period to renew it by mail had expired. So they had to get their photo retaken and schedule a time to go to the Post Office to fill out the paperwork. A thirty-minute activity on the computer turned into an entire morning of standing in line and filling out paperwork. That is similar to trying to find a new job after being fired-it's a whole lot harder.

Indeed, getting fired is not always entirely in your control, but just like getting hired, there is a lot you can do to help your case. Companies invest a lot of resources in finding and training workers, so firing people is usually very low on their list of priorities. There are usually two main reasons a person will get fired.

The Layoff

Businesses are entities subjected to forces outside of themselves. They expand and contract and are influenced by myriad variables. It is true that most businesses generally try to grow, sometimes to their detriment. With that said, through foreseen and unforeseen events, many often shrink. When businesses shrink, one way they stay alive and continue to exist as a business is to lay people off. Being laid off is not technically being fired, but it is also not a neutral activity. Being laid off has more to do with the business than the worker, but being laid off when your colleagues get to keep their jobs is a negative thing. The company says that they can only survive if they get rid of you. People laid off are usually the newest to the company ("last hired, first fired") or perform less essential jobs.

Interestingly, one can look at a company structure to guess how likely they are to get laid off if the company has financial trouble. Workers in companies that grow too fast, get acquired by other companies, or perform non-essential services are more likely to be laid off. Seasonal jobs (landscaping, farming) and volatile (manufacturing, refining) tend to see more layoffs than other jobs.

Being fired is not the end of the world, and if a business fires you, it would be better to have it be because they laid you off, but still, it's better not to get laid off. If you are fortunate to be choosing between multiple jobs, consider the likelihood of being laid off. For instance, I know many talented computer programmers who have had to choose between a job at a start-up and one at a more established tech company. Some prefer the start-up for the excitement and lack of corporate culture. Others choose the more established company for security and stability.

Getting Canned

Elsewhere I told a story about doing consulting at a software company that focused on training workers for the work world. During what turned out to be my final consultation, getting fired came up as the topic, and people told their stories of getting fired. I was surprised at one point when one of the trainers encouraged the trainees that getting fired was pretty standard, and it happens to everyone eventually. I broke into the conversation at that point and contradicted the statement. Getting fired is not normal. It's also not some mysterious experience that comes out of nowhere. All of the stories shared around that table were people doing obvious rule-breaking or failing to respond to corrections from supervisors.

Indeed, not all rule-breaking results in firing, but all people who get fired are often fired because of rule-breaking. There are heavy protections for workers against being unjustly fired in the US. There are also no restrictions on fired employees bringing lawsuits against offending companies. Even if courts dismiss these suits, they still require a lot of time and effort from the company to get dismissed. Due to the considerable investment it takes to train an employee, the potentially significant loss to the company and the ever-present risk of being sued, getting fired is usually a last resort. Companies will only do it when it costs more to keep you than to fire you.

Most managers and administrators I have worked with have a deep appreciation for the significance of getting fired. They know how costly it is, and so when a person has a "gap" in their resume or refuses to use a former manager as a reference, or the reference tells your potential employer that you were fired, this is a red flag. I would imagine it is such a bright red flag that most companies will not try to get more information from you about what happened that you got fired; they will simply pass on your application.

Most job coaches will give you the same advice if you get fired and start looking for a new job: be open and honest about it upfront. They give this advice because it is better for you to tell potential employers than for them to find out. And, as I said, there are lots of clues if a person gets fired. Practice telling someone you got fired and why the company fired you. You do not need to embellish the issue, and you certainly should not criticize the person who fired you. After all, everyone knows that it costs the company money to fire you, so telling a potential employer that you were fired unjustly or unfairly can be a bad idea (unless a court has determined that you were wrongly fired, of course). The potential employer will likely believe your former employer over you when stories conflict in this new hiring situation. So, say you were fired and give the reason for it. You should communicate that you "learned your lesson" and are a better worker because of the experience. You should have statements prepared about how you will avoid doing that thing you got fired for again.

John once told me he got fired for delegating his work to other people. Delegation is a great skill, but only managers and other authority figures can use it. John was delegating to his co-workers, over whom he had no authority. John reported he was not delegating out of laziness but efficiency and job satisfaction. He did not like some aspects of the work he was assigned, and a co-worker reported they liked it and seemed to be better at the job. So it made complete sense to John to delegate based on creating efficiencies and increasing enjoyment in work. The problem, of course, is that delegation is limited exclusively to people in charge, so John was justly fired for the act. At a later job interview, John talked about the situation to the potential employer and also recommended the potential employer call his former supervisor. When John got fired, he discussed his job performance with his supervisor, and it turned out that other than this obvious misstep, John had done an adequate job. The supervisor confirmed that John understood why he was being fired and could vouch for his understanding of the incident to future employers.

Companies usually request a job history and access to former employers when you apply for jobs. The shortest job history request I have seen has been past two jobs. Some ask for information from three to five past workplaces. Someone will eventually hire you after being fired, but they are taking a chance on you. Make it as easy as possible for them to justify hiring you by being transparent. Eventually, the firing incident will be off your record because you will have enough jobs in the past where you did not get fired. You will eliminate gaps in your resume and potentially problematic recommendations due to your mistakes. Again, not the end of the world, but getting fired is something you should avoid at all costs.

Observational Learning

One great thing about being a higher-level mammal is we can learn from the mistakes of others. Get people's stories about being fired. Look through the news and read about people who got fired. Find out what they did and for what reason. Examine your own decisions and motives, and find ways to improve your work performance to decrease the chance of being fired. Be polite, do your job, and ask for more work when you have finished.

Chapter 3

Employment Statistics

It's Bleak

Eighty percent of people on the spectrum are un- or under-employed. This number is an estimate and represents the best guess of employment gurus. The National Longitudinal Transition Study-2 (nlts2.sri.com) was completed in 2009 and generated some astonishing statistics. Sixty-eight percent of people between 16 and 64 work, while only 35% of people with any disability work. Thirty-two and a half percent of individuals with ASD work for pay compared to 59% of all respondents. Twenty-nine percent of young adults with ASD were looking for work if unemployed versus nearly 48% of all unemployed respondents looking for work.

There are more statistics, but none are better, and all suggest the same thing. If you have ASD, finding gainful employment is hard. If you are employed, it is likely that you are not making much or are working below your competency. However, I will also note that it's not necessarily the case that you will have a hard time finding work because you have a disability. Among disability groups, individuals with ASD had the second-lowest numbers regarding employment participation.

Reasons for Caution

Many factors influence these statistics. Because of some of the study's limitations, we have to be careful about how we read the numbers. For instance, there are likely people with autism that do not participate in these studies because they don't have a diagnosis. In addition, it is becoming more and more common for me to work with middle-aged professionals who are only achieving a diagnosis in adulthood. These are called "very late diagnoses" and used to be quite rare but are becoming less so. One of the reasons they did not have a diagnosis is because they did "good enough" in their formal education and early career. Something about their profile and the context allowed them to move through the system without getting flagged for evaluation. It's not always the case that these very late diagnoses people were exceptionally competent. Many of them grew up in a time when there were scarce resources for special education or significant stigma against neuro-diversity. Regardless, these people are not traditionally counted in such statistics because we don't know who they are, and they don't know or care to volunteer their information.

This study and similar studies are self-report. People are more likely to leave a review on Amazon if they have had a significant experience, either very good or bad. Therefore, I expect people with terrible experiences to be over-represented in these samples. I should point out, however, that the reported gaps in employment success between people with ASD and those without are about doubled, so we should still take them very seriously.

Statistics indicate that people with ASD seemed to respond better to employment intervention than other disability groups. So, despite having more bleak numbers, people on the spectrum seemed to have better numbers coming out of the intervention. They appeared to benefit more from intervention, meaning there's probably something to do about un- and under-employment for people with autism. This observation is one of the main inspirations for writing this current book. There's hope! There is something to do about it.

What can we do?

Below is by no means an exhaustive list, but if you are unemployed or under-employed, there are many things you can do.

Effort

The first disclaimer to what follows is that all the things that will get you a job, or a better job, will require effort. Much of my experience compels me to make this very clear to people – you will have to work to find work. Unfortunately, in my opinion, this is the first significant barrier to employment for people with ASD.

I usually find two main reasons for this reluctance to apply effort. First, many individuals with ASD came from an educational system that favored "accommodation" over "intervention." When my clients struggled to get 50 multiplication questions completed in five minutes in a timed in-class test, most of them had the number of questions they had to complete reduced or the time allotted increased rather than training to improve their time and accuracy. Question reduction and increased time are accommodations, and training in speed and accuracy is an intervention. I am not suggesting that one method for getting a child on the spectrum to succeed is necessarily better than another, but most strategies I see favor accommodation. This approach makes sense since accommodation is usually cheaper and more accessible than intervention. Unfortunately, most intervention teaches hard skills (like multiplication facts and how to excel at timed tests) and soft skills such as tenacity and persistence. You only build your ability to apply effort by doing challenging things.

Second, "doing better" requires work, and the lives of many people with whom I work are comfortable as-is, even if they are underachieving or unsuccessful. Many people I work with will say they would love to have a job or earn money, but they do not want to work for it. My old neighbor used to say, "Everyone wants a job, but no one wants to work." I think this reluctance to work is true for everyone, but I have never seen it embodied in a group of people as I have for individuals on the spectrum. I don't think people on the spectrum are more or less moral than any other group, but the commitment to only doing what they want seems to be a limiting factor for many when it comes to employment. Hence my disclaimer: dealing with your employment problem will require effort. You may decide that the required effort is too great or that your life is good as it is.

Employment Training

It is no surprise that people with ASD respond so well to basic employment training. I've seen this time and again in my work. When teachers highlight, teach, and practice fundamental concepts, people with ASD seem to pick them up quickly and apply them consistently. The work world is a rule-bound world. Work is managed and maintained by rules. Some of these rules are sophisticated, esoteric, and unspoken, but they exist and are quantifiable. There's a specific reason why putting your feet on the interviewer's desk means you will not get the job. Delegating jobs to your peers will get you fired consistently and predictably. If your boss is late to the meeting, it's understandable, and no explanation is needed (even if they give one). If you're late (i.e., the same behavior), you must explain why. No open-toed shoes, a rule often made fun of, has objective reasoning behind it.

The point is that people start learning these rules very early in childhood and continue learning them well into their careers. Most people I work with are surprised to hear that the work world is not chaotic but very orderly. They tell me about confusing or mysterious activities that happen at work or that they witness on TV, and we talk about why people find it funny, offensive, or expected. I point out that it is remarkable that people respond similarly to the witnessed behavior. This even response is evidence that the work world is orderly and rule-bound. You can learn and even master those rules and be successful at work.

Experience

Most of the work in your job for which you are evaluated is common to all jobs. People need to practice working. They can get this practice in part-time employment, volunteer positions, and internships as teens and young adults. When people are of working age, they need a full-time job to learn such skills. You practice this by getting up in the morning, going to work, and working all day without getting fired. Then you get up and go to work the next day and do the same thing. Do this about five days a week for a while, and you'll get much better at work.

You also need an actual skill set. That skill set will include specific hard skills, like engineering, deep frying McNuggets, open-heart surgery, and general hard skills like reading, writing, and math. People should go to school and not skip any steps. They should be in school with their peers as much as possible. This need for formal socialization means that taking a gap year or a break from education is rarely a great idea. Going "back" to school is much more strenuous than going to school.

Opportunity

I didn't get any formal employment help because I didn't qualify for any. I was too ordinary. I was a white, middle-class kid with average education, ability, and household income. I wasn't great at anything, but I wasn't terrible at anything. If I were anything different, even superfluously different, I would have qualified for assistance and taken it.

If you have an autism diagnosis in your formative education, you qualify for special education services. You (or your parents) should take everything the school offers you, and your parents should probably ask for even more. If you have an autism diagnosis in college, you qualify for disability services, and you should pursue the services. I tell my clients, "It's better to have them and not need them than to need them and not have them." Some people tell me they want to "see how it goes" without such services, and the reality is that the adult world was made by neurotypicals, for neurotypicals. It is already an unfair playing field if you have autism, so use the offered resources. Regarding employment, search for support through the county where you live or even look for companies trying to attract neurodiverse workers. Again, resources are out there, so take them all and use what you need.

Someone might feel like the things that I mentioned are obvious. So why do I need to put them in a book explicitly? It is true that once you see them, they are obvious. However, it's a pattern described by another author that I am applying to a specific population. Malcolm Gladwell's book <u>Outliers</u> (2008) nicely illustrates the above general points. He gives several examples of incredible success mediated by three mundane pillars: ability, hard work, and opportunity. He uses these pillars to explain the seeming outrageous success of outstanding individuals like Bill Gates and musicians like the Beatles. What can be done about the employment gap for individuals with autism also falls nicely in these three categories. Enhance and develop your abilities, apply effort, and take every opportunity offered.

Being Strategic

I think two common pieces of advice might be mucking up the education and employment process a bit for individuals on the spectrum: "Follow your dream" and "You can be and do whatever you set your mind to."

Follow Your Dream

Project-based learning has become a traditional pedagogy among educators. One version of this, I have heard, is to take the child's interest and use that interest to teach other skills. This approach makes sense since one of the barriers to education for many children is that the content is boring or unengaging. Some individuals take this further and suggest that educators direct children into careers that match their interests. Among individuals with autism, this has created a generation of children who want to grow up to be video game designers. Indeed, much of my work is coaching teens through the journey from video game lover to video game designer. Unfortunately, no one has followed me all the way along this journey. Becoming a video game designer is very hard, and designers have told me that the job is not all that great. It is certainly not playing video games all day. Others want to be professional E-sports competitors. Unfortunately, there is probably the same number of E-sports gigs as jobs being a professional basketball player, and no one is telling a child to be a professional basketball player. Telling a child to follow their dreams can make adults feel optimistic and helpful, and children smile when you tell them they can make money playing video games. This advice doesn't result in anything but disappointment, though. When I was growing up, my friend loved the show Knight Rider. In it, Michael Knight drove around in an indestructible and self-aware car named KITT and solved crimes for a wealthy benefactor. My friend was devastated to hear, later on, that there was no such thing as a self-aware car, and he was never going to look like David Hasselhoff.

I recommend countering the "follow your dreams" advice with "what abilities or experience do you have?" or "what would you like to do next?" Again, working in a grocery store in high school is an excellent experience for all teens, especially those on the spectrum, to learn about their abilities and interests and gain experience. My clients have found that they love working the register or dislike doing customer service. They like sitting down at a job or standing up. None of these aspects are dream-job aspects, but they are elements that matter to them in their work. We comb through feedback from the supervisor about skills to develop and talk directly about what sorts of activities they do and do not want in their next job. My former supervisor told me, "your next job should be better, in some way, than your current job." She rejected the notion of the "dream job" because it distracted her from finding the "better job."

You can be whatever you set your mind to be

No, you can't. Your employment options begin to be limited the moment you are conceived. Again, this is not necessarily bad news for people. Many people find that making decisions gets easier with fewer options. One limiting factor I have seen for people choosing a job or a career is too many good options. Even if you choose something arguably better, you are not choosing something that is also good. Rejecting good things is tough for people, so they often stay in a state of indecision for much longer than they should.

This tendency also explains why some people stay in bad jobs too long. Most people have at least one experience in their career where they knew they should get a different job or quit the one they had but didn't because it wasn't "bad enough." Even though we like to believe our options are unlimited, the reality is that we usually go with what is convenient, or being offered, or requires the least amount of effort. When it comes to choosing a career or a job, I encourage people not to spend too much time searching their imagination. I also encourage people not to focus too much on the effort of choosing. As I said earlier, the work world is a "work your way up" kind of place. Look for the job you can reasonably get and work toward getting better jobs. If you think you will somehow underachieve if you don't become a video game designer or E-Sports champion, reconsider the advice you received regarding your employment potential

People often criticize this advice and the way I present it as overly pessimistic. One can tone down some of the negativity by some wording changes. Still, I am offering these ideas the way I am to offset some of the overly idyllic and naïve language commonly used to prepare children and young adults for the work world. All people should work because there is an incredible benefit to working, but ultimately the work cannot only be about our desires. As described earlier, you work for a company. As a result, what you get from work is circumscribed and thus will not be all things to all people. Work will not ultimately meet all of your heart's desires. Even people looking for that dream job know that they will most likely settle for an approximation of that job. Or, if they get the dream job, how they feel about it might change over time. Pursuing your heart's desire and acting like you have unlimited resources to get it doesn't fit with the process of finding a job and working it. Such a directive can cause people to either pass on good opportunities or consider the sacrifice necessary to get and keep their heart's desire. Instead, I think it is good to look at your options (including experience, opportunities, etc.) and ask yourself which option you can optimize.

By the numbers

How do people make rational decisions about choosing a career? The answer to this usually involves executive functioning skills. I mean that you should gather and collate data to help inform your decision. Data gathering can help to reduce the overall number of options to choose from and decisions to make. This is important because a large volume of options tends to make people either put off a decision or use a strategy for decision-making that doesn't make sense and is useless. For instance, "what does your heart tell you?" is a decision-making strategy that is the focal point of nearly every children's movie made in the last 20 years but offers no practical or helpful advice for making major life decisions.

I encourage my clients to make a spreadsheet rather than just a Pros and Cons list. The problem with the Pros and Cons List is the high level of subjectivity involved. Also, the people I work with are so out of the box in their thinking that their Pro side and Con side are infinitely long and thus cannot be compared. I am suggesting here to formulate a discreet set of quantifiable variables that you can use to compare options. Making a spreadsheet can also be a review of values and resources. For instance, you might be able to look at the spreadsheet and decide that choosing between options might get more manageable if you had access to a specific resource (like a car). On the other hand, seeing your meager options laid out before you might encourage you to adjust your expectations about what sort of job you're willing to work.

What are the variables you can research and record?

Cost of education

It is a common belief that education is getting more and more expensive. The cost of living increases over time, and the cost of education would naturally increase as well. However, one should also consider other variables that affect the cost of education. First, there is usually a big reduction in cost for most colleges if you attend one in your home state. Private schools tend to be more expensive than public schools. Finally, many states are now offering free college education to their residents at Community Colleges (also called Junior Colleges). Education is increasing in price overall, but some institutions are lowering their tuitions. It is perfectly reasonable to choose a school based on price as the single factor. Research indicates a difference in quality between schools, but that difference is often negligible. For instance, the US's top 50 colleges and universities are roughly the same quality even though significant price differences exist. The overall good news for college students in the US is that the US has a very high standard for college education, causing most colleges to compare well to each other as far as quality of education.

The other thing to consider is what sort of employment potential you can expect when achieving your degree. Some educations cost more (e.g., medicine), but they also put you in jobs that earn more. Some cost a lot but qualify you for jobs where the pay is very modest.

Why is looking at cost important? Most people pay for college with loans from the government and private institutions. It has become customary for students to carry debt for many years when leaving college. The problem is that the debt to income ratio has been moving in favor of debt. For many people, this is artificially putting constraints on job prospects. For instance, people might choose a job exclusively for how much it pays. This method is a problem because there are a lot of other factors to consider. Also, someone might choose a job simply because their loans are coming due. They take the position not because it's a good job but because it's a paying job. Again, this artificially limits options and is initiated when you sign for your first college loan several years before. Second, when you are paying off debt, there are many good things you cannot buy, like a house or a car. Many people find they have to choose between debt and other things that build wealth (like retirement savings or financial safety nets), and again, you made this decision many years before when you signed the loan documents.

Interests vs. opportunity

What do you like to do or want to do? Is there an actual job that will pay you to do that? My favorite "what do you want to be when you grow up" responses have been "Alien Commander" and "Thinker." We have no definitive proof of aliens, so being their commander is not an option. Many people have reported that they want to be paid to think. This desire is like saying you want people to pay you to breathe. When I dig in, most people state they want to be paid to think about problems a business is having and solve them or think about new technologies or inventions. When I ask if they're going to be inventors, they say no. They just want to think about the invention and want others to make it.

Other people tell me they want to play video games for a living, be social media stars, or be movie directors. In general, most people I talk to choose careers with very few job opportunities. I encourage such people to look at the resumes of people they admire to see where they worked. For instance, Elon Musk was a programmer. Barak Obama has a law degree and was a community organizer. Einstein was a patent clerk. Lots of Olympians work at Home Depot. In addition to doing the things for which they became famous and admirable, these people had or have mundane jobs. What kind of job is related to your interest, even if not precisely, and is it plentiful? For example, many game designers choose programming jobs at tech giants, people interested in medicine choose nursing over being a physician, and physicists decide to teach because that is where the jobs are.

Isn't it more important for people to love what they do? What about motivating people by telling them to dream big? Again, this reasoning is like eating a candy bar right before the big game. You're energized for about 20 minutes and then dragging yourself around and hating your life for the next hour. People need substance in advice, not gimmicks.

Who you know

Most people have a story where they got a job they didn't deserve because of who they knew. For example, my Dad got me my first lawnmowing job. It was his friend's house, and I was eight years old. Upon reflection, it may not have been safe for me to be using power equipment due to my age, and if I had knocked on their door myself and asked to mow their lawn, they would have rightfully refused me. I've also taken terrible jobs because the people I worked for had influence and could open doors.

One of the first questions I ask when coaching a person about applying to college or looking for a job is, "who do you know?" Again, it can seem like this is contrary to the American Way. The American Way is to pull yourself up by your bootstraps; make your way; do everything independently without help. These sayings are terrible misperceptions of how things actually work. No one gets anywhere on their own. It's ok to highlight or favor specific employment options because you know someone with a connection to a job.

How is this good advice for people who traditionally have a problem with forming relationships? People who have autism are fully capable of developing relationships. However, it seems more challenging for them to form relationships than the average neurotypical person. Creating relationships is beneficial for people on many levels, not just for getting good jobs. Everyone you develop a relationship with to get a job has also benefitted the same way from such a relationship. We train children to be selfless in their dealings with others, but that's not what relationships are. We are interdependent people, meaning we take from others and others expect to take from us. The inverse is true in that we give to others and hope others give back to us. We have a perfectly reciprocal relationship in just this way of active give and take. It's called friendship, and it's self-governing in that when a friendship is no longer genuinely voluntary, it becomes something else. But friendship is just an example of inter-dependence in our culture. When I became a psychologist, my industry expected me to engage in the training and supervision of more junior psychologists (which I do). As a junior psychologist, I depended on that requirement, and I hope others expect that of me. We have numerous examples of relationships that rely on give and take, so yes, it is ok to develop a relationship with the expectation of getting something from it, like an advantage in getting a job or getting into college.

What are your needs/limitations

I think we should continually examine our flaws and shortcomings and work toward self-improvement. With that said, I believe there is a lot of freedom in admitting and accepting our limitations. One summer, I worked in a grocery store. It was quite possibly the worst summer of my life. I was in high school, and summers in Ohio can be brutal. I worked every summer from age eight, mowing lawns, landscaping, tree service, and construction. So I thought I would give the grocery store a shot. It was indoor work and thus airconditioned, better hours (landscaping is usually sun up to sundown), physically more manageable, and I would be working with many people my age. Most landscapers are older and angry. I got about 30 minutes into my first shift when I realized that I loved being outside, even when it was 95 degrees.

Some work may require abilities you lack; other work may show you what tasks you don't want to do. Some work might be disagreeable because of the conditions under which you have to perform it. Bad bosses or co-workers can ruin good positions. On the other hand, good bosses or co-workers can make bad jobs tolerable. One year, I had a clinic job where I got a new supervisor halfway through my term, and the job suddenly became intolerable. I think I have the intellect to be a lawyer, but I hear how lawyers talk to each other, and I can't imagine doing that all day, regardless of the pay. What do your experiences and self-knowledge say about what kind of job you can and cannot tolerate? Be careful about choosing work based on superficial factors like pay or temporary factors like fame. Research confirms that accepting and liking what you do are far more valuable.

Didn't I just say that money is a sufficient reason to choose a college? It's essential to look at what you're getting for your investment. Sometimes the investment is too high, and the compensation cannot match it. At the grocery store, I was more physically comfortable (compensation). Still, it turned out that I didn't mind the scorching heat, and I hated the monotony of the grocery store (investment). I could mow lawns for 10 to 12 hours with no problem. I couldn't bag groceries for longer than 30 minutes. It turned out that I preferred the company of my chain-smoking landscaping bosses to catty teenagers as well.

The step in between

You may decide that you cannot immediately do what you would like to do. For instance, I once worked with someone who decided he wanted to write and illustrate manga. The problem was that he could not speak Japanese. So, the correct answer for him was to apply to a college in Japan and learn how to speak, read and write Japanese to get a job with a manga publisher and work his way up. The people I talk to who want to "think" for a living need to go to college and get a degree in the industry for which they want to think. Alien Commanders probably have a background in history and are in the military. Finding the intermediary step to your future career is perhaps the most crucial part for most people. If your dream is to become a restaurant server, you can probably do that once you turn 16 and get your work permit. If you want to own a restaurant, you need to go to school to learn the culinary business. Most people want jobs that require preparation, so find out the relevant preparation and look for opportunities to do that.

On a personal note, when I was in elementary school, I was asked, along with 30 other classmates, to draw and title a picture of what I wanted to be when I grew up. I still have the picture somewhere. I wrote that I wanted to be an "author." I am an author now, but I didn't set out to be one. It turns out that I have little imagination, so my fiction writing is quite bad. I even studied English literature in college to no avail. Even though I was working toward a career from age eight, I didn't get my childhood dream job until my late 30s. Even now, I don't exclusively write books, but it is my goal to increase my writing. In my case, there were dozens of intermediary steps to get to where I wanted to go, and from here, there will be more steps to keep me moving in the right direction.

Employment stats

We have data on everything. If more information helps you make decisions, then the internet is the place for you. The Bureau of Labor Statistics[1] is an excellent place to start. You can find elementary statistics there, like the unemployment rate that can give you a sense of how easy or hard it will be to find a job overall (e.g., lower = harder, higher = easier) or look at numbers by profession. Salary is an important issue.[2] Some people I talk to have interests and skills in multiple areas and are looking for an industry with a lot of growth potential. Some are looking for job security (i.e., how likely it is to be able to stay in a job once you get it). Some want to capitalize on being a minority (e.g., my male friend chose nursing because he would

---

[1] https://www.bls.gov/

[2] https://www.bls.gov/bls/blswage.htm

become a gender minority and have better options). Many people don't want to work full time but want a professional-level job. Having a realistic sense of your options and then confirming your choices with data is available to anyone with access to the internet and a goal. But, again, the amount of data out there is considerable, and the risks of finding false and misleading data increase with the amount of time you spend looking for it.

Conclusion

Getting a job seems like a lot of work, doesn't it? It is, in fact. People don't like looking for work and will stay in bad jobs for longer than they should. It is also why this chapter focuses on practical, if not a little bit edgy, advice. The key is to keep moving forward because sometimes the right choice is the one that promotes action and momentum. And then, once you get that job, turn most of that energy toward doing your job the best you can (and some toward looking for an even better job).

Chapter 4

The Part-Time Job

It seems like part-time jobs used to be more common when I was a kid. I remember people having to give excuses for not having a part-time job during the summer. Every spring, my friends and I would scramble to find work that would start as soon as school got out. Some people would say they didn't have time for a job because they were in sports all summer. One friend traveled to Taiwan each summer to spend time with family, so he didn't work. No one ever said they passed on the part-time job to play video games or "hang out" or rest. Part-time work was something that teens and young adults in school full-time just did. How else were we supposed to get money for gas and pizza?

It is not hard to find both research studies and anecdotal reports about the value of part-time work for full-time students. Search "part-time-work-and-future-vocational-success," and a long list of articles and blog posts pop up, all adamantly favoring teens and young adults in school having part-time jobs. We now have decades of data to support the link between teens having part-time work and later vocational (career) success. For those who had part-time jobs, this is preaching to the choir. This chapter is a thesis in support of getting a part-time job.

Most of the articles you read will have a summary of the benefits of part-time work. However, at the top of the chapter, I will list some here to give some foundation for the detail I will share later on.

Money making

Making money is likely the primary reason your parent told you that you should want a part-time job. "Don't you have things you want to buy?" Most of my clients answer honestly, "no," and report that they have everything they want and having more stuff is not worth the effort to get it. My clients are correct in most regards. Most parents think about wants when it comes to spending money, and my clients think more about needs. My clients are intensely non-materialistic and monkish in their spending. "Walking around money" is not something they contemplate. But they should still want to have their own money. First, you need money to have "finances." Managing one's finances is complicated and requires training and practice. I have met many young adults who are ready for independence and have no idea if they even have a checking account or not. One man I was working with who was graduating college and about to start a full-time career-type job looked at his checking account and realized it was the kid's version of a checking account his parents opened for him when he was 10. Getting into your early to mid-twenties without basic information about managing finances is personally limiting. You need to make some money to start to learn how to manage finances.

Soft Skill Development

Years ago, I used to run a group for teens on developing independent living skills. One assignment I gave them was to ask their parents, between groups, about their first-ever paid job. Parents reported terrible jobs: cleaning toilets, carrying large objects, waking up at the crack of dawn to shovel snow, and on and on. No one ever came back with a story about the parent's first job being their current job. No one ever had a story where the first job was anywhere related to their eventual career. Yet all the parents talked about how useful the first job was to their current career success. How can this be?

All jobs train people in soft skill development. Soft skills, as opposed to hard skills, are those skills that apply to all jobs. They include getting along with co-workers, doing thorough work, being on time for work, and working when told to work (regardless of how you feel about it). I can trace many of my current daily work practices back to my early days of mowing lawns with my brother. I should also note that I have had co-workers with limited or no work experience, and the learning curve is very steep for them. They struggled with things I found simple, like getting to work on time every morning.

Nevertheless, being exposed to work expectations and developing soft skills in a low-stakes environment has enormous benefits for everyone who eventually has to work. I recall marveling at some of my professors in university who could not seem to be on time for the class they were teaching. What a shame. They were brilliant, wonderful people who couldn't get their act together. It was as if they'd never been fired from a job at McDonald's for being late the final time.

Experience

I am about halfway through the summer and halfway to starting a new school year as I'm writing this. Some kids I work with, at my advice, began looking for summer jobs several weeks ago. Some got interviews, and all of them reported that employers asked about their job experience. One admitted that he gave the wrong answer of "none." He responded that he had never had a part-time job before, so therefore the correct answer was that he had no experience working. Not surprisingly, he didn't get the job. We talked about his past experiences that might map nicely onto the job he was applying for. Thankfully it was in food service, so he could at least talk about setting the table for dinner, doing some of the cooking for himself and his family, and the like. The benefit of getting a part-time job is that no one has to wonder if you can work. Work experience is the most basic expected experience for any job.

"Can you work?"

"Yes, sir. As a matter of fact, I used to work, so I have a history of working. It says so on my resume."

"Great, you're hired!"

The primary thing employers are looking for is actual work experience. It is true that if you apply for a job mowing lawns, it is ideal if you've mowed a lawn before. Before you go to that interview, you should mow a lawn. But ultimately, many employers are willing to train you to do a specific job, like using the friers to make hush-puppies. They will be very hesitant to teach you to work. Your resume should tell them you already know how to work, regardless of the specific job.

Exposure

Understanding the work world can be very difficult for a person who has never worked. It can be hard to imagine an employer telling you to do something and then expecting you to do it right away every time. It can be tough to imagine an employer wishing you to do something that doesn't immediately and directly benefit you. It can be tough to imagine an environment with zero tolerance for disrespect and a lousy attitude. It can be tough to imagine an environment where threats are not only ineffective for getting your way but will always lead to you losing something important (i.e., getting fired). Work is different from home, even if you have chores. Work is different from school, even if you have homework experience. You just have to be there to have any context for the work world.

It's like death and taxes

Work is inevitable for everyone. If a person chooses not to work, it's not like society will say, "Ok, have a nice life. See you on the other side." People who don't work don't have a society. Working is necessary to be a part of society. Indeed, as hard as it is to work, it's harder to be outside society. Everyone has to work, so choosing not to work is nothing more than an act of procrastination. Elsewhere I've written that I have been amazed at meeting people who believe(d) that not working was an option they could choose. This belief is a false and made-up narrative that society does not support. So, if you decide not to work, not only are you outside of society, but you're stuck in a dream world where reality will forever be nonsensical.

One could say more of the above points, but none can be reasonably refuted. Each is sufficient to support the claim that teens and young adults in full-time school need part-time work.

Are you supporting child labor?

My audience lives in places with stringent rules about child labor, so I don't worry about readers taking my message in a way that would hurt or disadvantage children. States in the US require a certain minimum age for children to work and limit the amount and types of work they can do. Outside of this, it is common for children to be paid for extra chores or helping out neighbors. Parents have the initial responsibility to train their children to work. Generally, parents start with routine duties and then graduate to more time-intensive or necessary chores for extra pay. Ideally, when a 16-year-old applies to their first job, they should be able to say that they have been working for their parents and neighbors doing "odd-jobs" for a while. At least one neighbor would be willing to write a letter that the applicant is hardworking and dependable.

Some parents tell me that their adolescent or young adult child has never worked or had chores. If this is your situation, then today is the day. Many parents sign their children up for volunteer positions to build that work ethic. You might put this book down right now and write out a chore chart that includes a couple of daily and weekly chores. Today is the day.

How to get a part-time job

When I lived in San Francisco, I would tell my clients who asked, "where do I look for a job?" to get on the bus at the stop closest to their house and look for Help Wanted signs in the windows of stores the bus passed. I would tell them to set an alarm for 20 minutes and when the alarm goes off, exit the bus at the next stop, cross the street, and look at the other side of the road for signs on the bus back to their house. The good news about a part-time job is that people don't expect you to have a specific skill set, for the most part. You are qualified for just about any part-time job out there. If you were looking for a professorship at a university teaching and researching child psychology, you would have to do a nationwide search. Part-time work flipping hamburgers is the same on the East Coast as it is on the West Coast and everywhere in between. Part-time work is usually right there in your neighborhood.

Job Search

Get on the bus and look, look in the newspaper, and look online. Type in "part-time-job" and your zip code into an internet search engine and see what comes up. Ask your parents if they know anyone who has a business that is hiring or could hire a part-time worker. My mom or dad has found many jobs I have worked. These are good jobs to start because your parent essentially vouches for you, which can serve as a reference. Some people I know want to do the job search entirely independently, which I understand. To them, I say that finding a job, and especially a first job, is a specific skill and one where most veteran job-seekers welcome any extra help. I mean that it is no exceptional accomplishment to get the job independently. The accomplishment is working the job.

The application process

You should plan to apply to several jobs at the same time. Making multiple applications is standard practice. If you end up accepting a job, and then another job place calls you for an interview, simply tell them that you were already hired and thank them for replying to your application. You should apply to multiple jobs at once because the application process can take anywhere from a day to several weeks. For example, most people looking for a summer job only plan to work for eight to 12 weeks, so if you spend two to four weeks looking for that job, you've lost between 17% and 50% of your summer work time. That's a lot of walking around money.

If you want to start working on June 1, you should start the job search process closer to May 1. It is ok to tell employers that you can begin to work right when school lets out. Again, this is standard practice and will not typically hurt your chances of getting a job. On the contrary, it can send a positive message to employers that you can plan and are eager to work. The short of it is that you should not start looking for work when you can work. Instead, you start looking for a job about two to four weeks before you can work.

Write a resume. A resume is a formal list of your work experience and education. The resume also has basic contact information about you. Since the resume is a formal document, avoid putting too much personality into it. For most people applying for part-time work, the resume will be no more than a page long. Your resume might be a half-page long. Still, you should have one. There are many free online resume builders from which to choose. In addition, there are professional resume writers you can hire and computer programs you can buy to help you write resumes. For a person making their first resume, ask your parents or teacher for help with creating a resume. My current resume looked much like my first boss's resume when I graduated college. After seeing my application for the job (for which he hired me), he recommended I make my resume more professional-looking and offered his own as a template. I have since shown mine to early-career psychologists for the same reason. Once you create your resume, you should immediately update it with new, relevant information and get rid of old, outdated, or irrelevant information. For instance, once getting a job, add that position to your resume. Once you complete a school year or graduate from school, add that information to your resume. Have people look at your resume from time to time and give you their impressions and advice.

Complete the application, either online or in-person, thoroughly and with care. Ask someone to look at what you have written and comment on it. Type out your responses instead of writing by hand, if possible. If not, you can have someone else fill it out if their handwriting is better. Keep a copy of the application because most applications ask the same questions and for the same information.

Whenever you go into the place you want to work, to pick up or drop off the application, you should be polite, make good eye contact, speak clearly, and look clean and neatly dressed. If you cannot do all of these things to at least a basic degree, you may want to wait to present yourself. Do not underestimate the importance people place on the "first impression." How you act and appear has a lot to do with your chances of getting a job. Applicants should know that almost all employers will trust the impression they get of you when first meeting and interacting with you. Establishing an impression is the primary role of the interview – to "get the feel" for what kind of person you are.

Interestingly, research suggests that the interview doesn't add much to the employer's ability to predict your success as an employee. Even so, the potential employee's "impression" is crucial in the hiring process. I would suggest that the impression one gives might even be more motivating to the employer than the applicant's actual work experience.

There are things to do in the time between submitting the application and attending an interview. Specifically, the applicant should become familiar with the place they hope to work. They might gain this familiarity by looking a company up online and reading about the history of the company. Further, it could also mean going to the store and noticing the qualities of the workplace. Do their employees seem happy or friendly? Do you even like the product they sell? Obviously, this leads to other practical advice. Apply at places where you shop (or would shop if you had money). If you dislike burritos, don't apply for a job at a burrito shop. If you think Walmart has too large a carbon footprint, don't apply for a job there.

The Interview

Most jobs will invite you for an interview. Again, the most helpful information for employers seems to be the resume. Research suggests the resume is the best predictor of future job success based on work history. Regardless, the in-person interview is a staple of the job hiring process. It is also traditional and formulaic. To that end, you can prepare for the job interview and improve your performance in the interview. It is possible to be qualified for the job you are applying for, be the best candidate for the job based on your resume, and still not get the job due to poor performance in the interview. What I just said contradicts research, but it demonstrates the importance of the job interview.

It is essential to know what the interviewer is looking for in the interview. More important than the answers to the interview questions are how you answer the questions. Said another way, the interviewer pays more attention to the "how" than the "what" of responses to questions.

How does the applicant present?

Are they polite and respectful to authority? Do they understand the norms of the hierarchical work environment? Do they know how to dress appropriately? Do they know the proper tone to use in a professional setting? Do they seem to understand the questions asked?

Is there anything strange, offensive, or off-putting about the interviewee? Is there anything weird, offensive, or off-putting about their responses to questions or conversations? Do they seem like they want the job?

I have talked with many people who interview and hire new employees. In addition to gathering specific information about the interviewee to determine whether or not they are fit for the job, all interviewers report that they get a general "sense" about an applicant in the interview. An interviewer can get three broad categories of sense: good, bad, and mixed/unclear. You want the interviewer to get a "good sense" about you, not a "bad sense." If an interviewer gets a "mixed sense" about you, that can help them choose between you and an equally qualified interviewee for whom they have a "good sense." Most interviewers trust their ability to "get a sense" about an applicant from an interview and ask questions and make statements (to see how you will react) to help them form that sense. Polite, cheerful, engaging, interested, alert, competent: these are all qualities an applicant can communicate verbally and non-verbally throughout the interview to help solidify the "good sense" category in the mind of their interviewer. I guess that politeness might be the top one they are looking for in those qualities. Indeed, competent, alert, interested, engaging, cheerful, but impolite would likely lead to no job offer.

The Interview Questions

You should research the place where you are interviewing. You should understand what they do and how they do it before attending the interview. The following are some common questions to expect for the interview. Of course, this is not a comprehensive list, but remember that the interviewer is trying to "get a sense" or form an impression of you. They are looking for you to fall solidly into the good or bad category because this makes their job of hiring the right person easier. Make it easy for them to get a good sense of you by preparing and practicing some responses to these questions. I'll list the question and then explain why it is such a common question and how one might think of approaching it. The best response you can give to these questions is a genuine, direct, and personal (i.e., specific to you) response.

Do you have any experience?

This question seems like a yes/no question, but it's either a yes or I'm not hiring you question. In a part-time job, you are unlikely to be interviewed unless you at least have a chance of getting hired. Consider the job you are applying for and what types of work it entails, and then look for both hard and soft skills about which you can talk. Have you ever pushed a broom (janitorial), microwaved something (food preparation), used a tool (all jobs have some sort of tool), or done what someone told you to do (taking orders, task completion)? The only acceptable response to this question is yes, so you need to pull something that counts as experience from your life.

With that said, I suspect some people out there genuinely have no experience because they have been waited on hand and foot and have no obligations or expectations placed on them. If this is you, you need a chore list immediately, and it should include a variety of tasks, from cleaning to cooking or running errands. You should also immediately look for a volunteer position to experience oversight that is not your parents.

What are your strengths and weaknesses?

Above is an old and much-maligned question, but I recently talked to a teen who was asked a version of this question. The question ultimately gets at self-knowledge. How well do you know yourself, and how coherently can you talk about yourself? This question is not about bragging or self-defamation. The question is seeking evidence that you can think about yourself and your work at a basic level. Employers know that the ability to think about yourself in context is essential. Here's the key, though. You need to respond to this question not with what you like or dislike about yourself so much as what others would praise or criticize. For example, "I am really good at math" is an ok response, but "I get good grades in math" is better. Both may be true, but the second one (about grades) means that others think you're good at math too.

Someone might wonder if talking about your weaknesses is a trap. It's not. The truth is that we all have flaws. The problem is not that you have them but that you're not aware of them. Evidence that you cannot critically evaluate yourself or that no one has critically evaluated you is a red flag for employers. That gets you bumped out of "good sense."

What makes you interested in this job?

Even if they don't ask this question, you need to think deeply about this one. With the part-time job, it's ok to say that it's close to your house or you want to make money. No one expects every cashier working at McDonald's to be passionate about McNuggets (even if it's true). Suppose you love McNuggets, though, consider applying for work at McDonald's. You should be ready for this question because you will have a hard time hiding your disinterest in the company or the product in an interview. A careless attitude is not attractive. Note that the opposite of careless is not desperate. Interested, eager, motivated, you need to stoke these feelings in yourself about this job before you attend the interview.

Have you ever heard the story about the guy who walked into McDonald's, and the person at the cash register said, "You're here more than me. You should work here."? This is the right idea. Where should you apply for work? If you can choose, apply to places you shop or stores you like. Employers like to hear that you are in their store all the time, enjoy the product, or otherwise appreciate the company or organization's work. But, again, it's also ok to say that the place is easy to get to (meaning, you'll be on time and dependable) and the pay is proper (meaning, you have some financial goals and will show up for every work shift).

Do you have any questions for me?

The answer to this question is yes. It's always yes. You ask questions about things you find essential. Your response to this question will tell the interviewer what you focused on in preparation for the interview. It will also tell them what you focused on during the interview. Finally, it will say to them that you are competent (competent people ask questions and don't pretend they know everything), paying attention, interested, engaged, and polite. It is very reinforcing for people to "share attention." When we're children, we show our parents the drawing we made, and both you and the parent enjoy the fact that you appreciate the same thing simultaneously. It is satisfying to the interviewer when you ask for clarification or more information about something they said (because you were thinking about it while they were talking about it). Remember that they work for that company too, and asking questions can signal (correctly, I hope) that you also want to work for the company they value.

Make sure the questions are appropriate and topical. Be careful about asking questions about content that was not at least alluded to in the interview (e.g., job-related). An excellent skill for social interactions is asking people questions about their experiences or opinions. People like to know people are paying attention to them and interested in them.

What if, you might ask, the interviewer answers all of the questions you had? You should mention that that is the case and give an example. For instance, you might have asked how many hours employees work, and the interviewer talks about that explicitly. Tell the interviewer that you had that question, but they answered it well. Some interviewers will ask if you have any "more" questions. Reference to "more" questions usually signals the end of the interview. In certain countries, and even to an extent here in the US, when you've finished your meal at a restaurant, paid the check, and decided to sit and talk with your friends, waiters will ask you if you want "more" water. That is a signal it's time to leave. Same with the interview if it's gone on a while.

Post Interview

Sometimes the interviewer offers you a job right there. If you like the job, you are welcome to accept it. Often interviewers will say they "will let you know" soon if they want to hire you. Very seldom will interviewers tell you right there that they do not want to hire you.

If you have to wait to hear if they want to hire you, consider having a follow-up communication with the interviewer. For instance, if you can communicate by email, send an email that thanks them for the interview and offer to answer any other questions they may have. This email is polite behavior and also shows interest in the job and knowledge of basic social norms. Some companies ask applicants not to follow up after applying or after the initial interview. It's a "don't call us; we'll call you" approach, which is fine. Some jobs get so many applications that they would never get to the hiring if everyone followed up. Do not follow up when it's explicitly stated not to. You should follow up sometime between 24 hours and one week. No sooner or longer.

With that said, some businesses will wait longer than a week to contact you about whether or not you got the job. A couple of jobs where I applied took six months to follow up. Many simply never followed up. This experience is also why you should apply for multiple jobs at once. You will note that a minority of jobs are very long in following up or simply never get back to you. It is impolite, in my opinion, but it is a reality. It's also the case that you probably don't want to work for them anyway.

Take the job

If you get offered the job, you should take it. I remember foolishly thinking that everyone wanted to hire me and maybe there would be a bidding war for my services. No one has ever expressed that kind of interest in me for anything. The average person should probably take the job offered.

You should also immediately update your resume and think about the next job you want. It is improbable that your first job will be your last job. It is doubtful that your first job will even be good. Remember, these are the kinds of people, and this is the kind of job that will hire you. Take the job, update your resume, build your skills, gain a good reputation, and get a better job the next time you apply.

Chapter 5

Your Co-workers

Your most vital social influence as an adult may be the collective impact of interactions with your co-workers. Because of this, you must have more than a basic understanding of a co-worker.

Simply put, co-workers are those you work with who are not your boss. They fill the category of peer, but the nature of your relationship with them is peculiar. So let's talk about who these people are.

When you are sitting at your desk, you will interact with several different groups of people. The people you will interact with that are not your co-workers are your superiors (those in charge of and responsible for you) and people generically described as customers or people who buy things from the company you work for. Someone can have lower status than you yet be your co-worker. When you become responsible for the work of another person you are no longer co-workers. If you are responsible for another person's work, you are that person's superior, and you are not peers. For many people, the co-worker will be the most populated subgroup in the society of your office. When you look up from your desk, you will spot a co-worker.

Compared to other relationships you might have had, the co-worker is most closely related to the classmate. However, this comparison is imperfect because the nature of your "work" is fundamentally different when you are a worker as compared to a student. As stated in Chapter 1, the world of schooling is all about the student. In the work world, it's all about the company (and not the individual worker).

You may have multiple relationships with any of your co-workers, but the primary relationship will most likely be that of a co-worker. Most adults will identify some co-workers as friends, but the primary relationship is that of a co-worker even then. Interestingly, when people stop being co-workers, as in the case where people quit their job and work somewhere else, this act can either destroy or enhance the friendship aspect of the relationship. The friendship is destroyed through inattention and lack of maintenance in most cases.

One principle governs the co-worker relationship: how does this co-worker affect my ability to do my job? Conflict occurs when people see their co-workers getting in the way of being successful at their jobs. A co-worker making it hard for someone to do their job should seem absurd and contrary. After all, they work for the same company and ultimately have the same goal, do they not? Everyone working for the company should have the same ultimate goal to support the company's health. This statement illustrates the difference between the work world and the school world. The reality of the work world is far from this. Most larger workplaces have Human Resources (HR) departments that aim to support the co-worker relationship and a cooperative work environment. Most decision-making in HR is driven by a distinctive ratio of rationality and emotionality. People on the spectrum tend, in my experience, to weigh heavily on rationality when it comes to decision-making. Most co-workers, however, are more balanced in their decision-making between rationality and emotionality. If all people were aligned in their decision-making, there would be far less conflict to manage at work (and less need for HR). Many of my clients criticize people for being too emotional (and thus irrational) about the problems at work. Still, the truth is that if my clients were more balanced between rationality and emotionality, there would also be less conflict at work. It's not that rationality is superior to emotionality or vice versa; the problem is that people have different ratios of the two options in various situations. Human Resources is the department in most workplaces that helps sort out disputes that arise from this lack of balancing of the ratios between two or more co-workers operating in the same context.

Like it or not, we cannot help but blend the co-worker relationship with other relationships. Humans cannot limit their appreciation for their co-workers exclusively to the aspects of the person that have to do with work production. There is both an active and a passive process that drives the development of our relationship with our co-workers.

Passively speaking, many people spend more awake time with their co-workers than even with family members. This fact should seem absurd since we love our family members and may even dislike our co-workers, but spend more time with those we dislike. Spending so much time together makes it hard to hide or obscure aspects of our values, preferences, and personality. Humans quickly develop and engage in habits and routines that ultimately point to our priorities. Your co-workers will learn about you extensively from being around you while you engage in your habits. Your co-workers might know more about your likes and dislikes than your family members. Humans cannot help but broadcast information about themselves, even information they don't have conscious access to themselves. This process is passive because people observe you engage in habits and routines that you do not intend to be self-expressive. These patterns and routines allow people to peer deep into your psyche and know things about you that you may not be aware of yourself.

The active process is something that confuses many of my clients. People, in general, like to know things about the people they spend so much time and with whom they share goals. The magazine rack at the grocery store suggests we also like to see a lot about people with whom we spend no time. Further, interest in fanfiction means we want to know a lot about people who don't even exist. The thoughts, feelings, preferences, hopes, and all sorts of internal, private, and even hidden aspects of a person are the most exciting things to people about other people. Your co-workers are intensely interested in you as a person (even if they dislike you), and they become more interested in you the longer you work together. I think this desire to know more about people comes from an internal drive for people to affiliate with each other. Knowledge forms the basis for trust, and trust is the foundation for solid groups of people. Humans have created groups called societies since at least the beginning of recorded history, and likely earlier than that. Grouping seems to be part of our nature, and there is absolutely something instinctive in people to wonder about the internal processes of other people. When we see someone do something seemingly irrational or dangerous, we ask, "What were you thinking!?" Most people are not satisfied just seeing the behavior; we want to know the thought that drove it.

The Water Cooler

I just wrote about 1200 words. It took me about 45 minutes to write that much. When I got to the end of the section, I needed a physical and mental break. My knees were tight, so it felt good to stand up, and I wanted to shift my thinking away from the co-worker's description to a discussion of the water cooler. If I worked in a traditional office (I work by myself), I would have walked over to the water cooler to get a drink. But I would have walked there not just for the water, but as part of an informal but scripted social activity common in workplaces.

A water cooler's purpose is evident in its name-it is a container of chilled drinking water for the delight and refreshment of the drinker. The water cooler is a metaphor for a place where the formality of a workplace is relaxed, and people can be more informal. "Water cooler talk" is precisely the use of informal language to discuss less formal topics and specific topics that have little to do with actual work. Gossip is a form of water cooler talk. In water cooler conversations, people commonly ask co-workers about what they do when they are not at work. "How was your weekend?" is the water cooler talk on Monday morning. Upon exiting a formal work meeting, people will gather at the water cooler to ask each other's opinions about the meeting. Was it a good meeting or a bad one? Views about the meeting usually have little to do with completing work. Still, most people value this information because it's an internal experience of another person they cannot readily know. Water cooler talk can build people's understanding of each other. That knowledge builds trust, which can produce the strength of the group. Water cooler talk can benefit the company, which is why it is not only tolerated but, in many cases, encouraged. Let's look at examples.

Many people have formal breaks during the day. For example, when I worked at the grocery store, I had two 15-minute breaks and a 30-minute lunch. During these breaks, water cooler talk happens, and most people find informal conversation relaxing and enjoyable. Some will avoid such conversations because of personal discomfort, and others avoid such water cooler talk to prevent getting to know their co-workers. Indeed, some people only want to have a formal, work-based relationship with their co-workers. To accomplish this, they will avoid informal contexts with their co-workers. The reasons a person wants to maintain the formality of the relationship can vary, but in general, it is considered odd and rude. Avoidance of such talk can lead to a strain on the co-worker relationship.

It used to be more popular to smoke cigarettes, so there was an activity called the "smoke break." I never smoked, but co-workers still invited me to attend smoke breaks. As a landscaper, I discovered that many people chose to landscape so they could smoke whenever they wanted to. Since they were almost always outside, there were no prohibitions against smoking. Lighting a cigarette signaled even less formality with my landscaping co-workers. Landscapers traditionally rejected many formalities at work in general. Interestingly, one of the only rock-solid rules in these highly informal work settings was deference to authority. People still got fired for being disrespectful to the boss.

Many co-workers celebrate the end of the formal part of their workday by actively engaging in an informal part of the day, specifically with co-workers. Traditionally, people's workday would end at 5 pm, and co-workers would immediately travel to a bar or restaurant. It's interesting that since they were "off the clock," they could celebrate the end of the workday with anyone they wanted to. They could even be alone since they had been around people all day. Instead, this tradition of meet-me-at-the-bar-after-work was formed and is still popular, especially as the weekend approaches (and the number of hours spent together is at its height!). This tradition is still water cooler behavior.

Finally, on a personal note, I worked for a landscaping crew that had a tradition called "hot laps." Near the end of the day, we would all pile in the work trucks and drive around, admiring our work. Even though we had just spent a lot of time together (in summers, we would work while it was light, so up to 14 hours a day), we still wanted to create a more informal atmosphere and admire the product of our shared work. We would talk about plans for the evening or things that happened during the workday that were too casual for discussion during the more formal work time. This conversation was also water cooler talk, and the purpose was to build knowledge and solidify our group.

So how does one manage these water cooler situations? First, it is essential to note what behavior signals a group is switching from formal to informal and back. Some workplaces are more structured so that casual conversations happen only during scheduled break times. Some signals are much more subtle, so I recommend the novice or "new guy" be in a formal mode at all times in the beginning. Note when people start to talk about things that have nothing to do with work. Informal topics that reveal little new information may be tolerated in formal environments. For instance, a co-worker, seeing a box of donuts in the breakroom, states he likes donuts. This statement signals it is appropriate to speak informally but on a very surface level. When people begin to discuss emotions, this becomes a deep informal discussion. As I said above, people cannot help but form habits and routines, so be on the lookout for the signals to happen at routine times.

Be wary if you think your boss is signaling water cooler talk with you. Informality between bosses and subordinates is much more taboo than between co-workers. I would argue that there is never the co-worker informality achieved between bosses and their subordinates. Formality, on some level, always presides over these hierarchical relationships. "It's lonely at the top" describes the lack of opportunities for informality as a person moves up in management and responsibility. Eventually, you have no peers you work with because your peers are other company executives. It gets lonely. Sometimes your boss will ask your opinion (an internal experience that people do not readily know), but that opinion should always be related to work or support productivity. Even very socially adept people have ventured into informal interaction with their boss and had it unexpectedly worked against them. As a general rule, I would encourage my clients to never have water cooler talk with their superiors, even if the superior seems to want such informality.

Like I said, not engaging in water cooler talk can be seen as strange or even hostile by co-workers, so it is something that my clients should intend to do, even though the process can be mysterious and mistakes can be costly. Water cooler talk generally moves from shallow to deep. This movement reflects the general nature of all relationships over time. The longer we know and interact with people, the deeper the relationship becomes. With some exceptions, if the process of deepening the relationship happens too quickly, people can become uncomfortable. Most people have a sense of the current depth of the relationship and the expectations for what is appropriate to reveal to another person at that depth. Further, most people know that increased depth is an expectation, so they will experiment with what information will serve to increase the depth of the relationship and at what speed. Most people who do this worry if what they are sharing is "too much too soon" but will also proceed on an intuitive level. They just know if it's too much. Often, we will also consult others and get their opinions if the depth and speed of sharing information are in question.

If you are asking, "how much is too much too soon?" or even thinking you have no idea what I am talking about, I recommend you evaluate the depth of the relationship from the content people are sharing with you. You can judge the content by how readily knowable the information is versus unknowable. Emotions are deeper (unknowable) than preferences. "I am angry" is revealing more unknowable information than "I like the color red," even though both represent thoughts. My best advice for managing these water cooler conversations is to talk about what other people are talking about and match the content and quality (i.e., depth) of the information they are sharing. Better yet, ask people about themselves. "How was your weekend? What did you end up doing?" If your question is a good one, people will reciprocate and ask you the same thing. Or, if people ask you a question, you should ask it back to them. This reciprocation is suitable for managing water cooler talk. You need a basic understanding of the purpose and the mechanics and then apply a few rules to it, specifically matching the quality of another person's statements and reflecting questions. As people practice water cooler talk and pay attention to how people are responding to them, they can develop a more intuitive sense of interaction, and it becomes easier.

Snitch, Whistleblower, Advocate

A client once told me that when he went to college, he was given the nickname "The Sherriff" by his suitemates. He told me he was initially honored by the nickname, and then someone was able to describe to him why it was not a desirable name. Initially, he felt honored to be aligned with those whose job is to serve and protect. Eventually, he realized that no one in the suite thought it was appropriate for him to be in that role. They didn't want to be served and protected by him. He had inadvertently stepped into the role in a different capacity-an unwanted, despised, dripping faucet of incessant and unnecessary reminders of the rules. They were worried that The Sherriff would tell on them to the real police.

Snitches, whistleblowers, and advocates all share the activity of disseminating information to authorities. A person can share precisely the same information and be called any of these three names. What results in the name they get has to do with context and perspective. Yet these are not the same title. One you never want to be called, the other you should dread having to be called, and the last you should desire to be called. So let's talk about each one.

Never be called a snitch

I remember it was cool to say, "snitches get stitches." No one I knew ever gave anyone stitches for being told on, but the point is that if you make something terrible happen to me (i.e., get me in trouble by telling on me), I'm going to make something terrible happen to you in return. Snitches get stitches all the time in TV shows and movies.

Snitching is always a derogatory term. In movies, snitches are criminals or people engaged in criminal activity who agree to give the police information about other criminals for a lighter punishment. Snitches get caught by police for a crime (usually because they are careless or dim-witted). They then will "sell out" their criminal friends to avoid full responsibility for their behavior. Snitches are seen as underhanded and untrustworthy, even by the people they are snitching to (i.e., the police).

"I'm telling on you" is a type of snitching behavior. You will hear this on the playground with little children when they don't get their way or the intentional misbehavior of others makes them uncomfortable. Most children quickly learn that "telling on people" is a bad thing, even if what they are reporting is the bad behavior of others. The line between snitching/telling on someone, and self-advocacy is challenging for all people to judge, yet judge we must, since no one likes a snitch. Also, I know from experience that the line between snitching and informing is solid and definable. Some snitches get stitches, but mostly snitches get left out of things and ignored. Don't ever get the title of snitch because it is a tough one to lose.

So, what's the difference between telling on someone and advocating for yourself? This distinction is relevant in the world of the average gangster and the playground, and it also tends to play out in the work world. If there is a problem you can or should be able to deal with yourself, you should try to address it yourself without the help of an authority. If you take one of these situations you can or should be able to handle on your own and bring an authority in to handle it, it's called snitching or telling on someone. If the situation is truly out of your control, bringing in an authority to manage it is called advocacy. So the line between the bad (snitching) and the good (advocacy) is not only what a person can handle on their own; it's what others reasonably think they should be able to handle on their own. Many of my clients find themselves overwhelmed in many interpersonal situations and determine that they need to bring in an authority. The problem is that the people around you decide whether or not your behavior is telling on someone or advocating for yourself. In this case, it is not what you can or cannot handle but what an average person can handle. Unfortunately, many of my clients become disadvantaged because attentive parents or professionals manage their interpersonal problems so that they do not have practice of skill to manage for themselves. Professionals can over-advocate for people to their detriment.

People can indeed unjustly label others a snitch. However, the standard for this label is not a single individual but what the group decides. So, if one person sees you as a snitch, that doesn't necessarily mean the group does. Generally, it's what the group decides that's most important regarding your reputation. Beware, however, the individual that sees you, even unjustly, as a snitch. They can still respond with "stitches."

Dread being called a whistleblower

Whistleblowers are those who inform individuals or organizations of illicit or illegal activity. For example, whistleblowers brought down Big Tobacco. Companies that pollute the environment are often brought down or brought to justice by whistleblowers. Some laws protect whistleblowers from being treated poorly by their employers or the government.

So why should you dread being called a whistleblower? Despite ultimately serving the public good, the entity giving you stitches (and they will give you stitches) is no longer an individual but a corporation. Usually, the corporation is massive and very powerful. Whistleblowers are required when such large entities need to be brought to justice because the entities have generally used their incredible power and authority to divert attention away from their wrongdoing. When they are found out, or might be found out, this incredible influence can be directed exclusively at the whistleblower.

Even though the stitches are unjust, and even though the corporation will pay for those stitches (usually), the stitches still do significant damage to the individual. Bringing corporations to justice is extensive, slow, and rarely ever just. Meanwhile, the whistleblower still needs to make a living, pay a mortgage, and raise children. The whistleblowing process is incredibly disruptive to an individual's life.

If a situation comes up where you can be a whistleblower, it is just to take on that role. Because of the possibility of disruption in a person's life, no one should ever look for opportunities to be a whistleblower.

In my line of work, I have the opportunity to inform on people (sometimes I am legally compelled to do so) involved in wrongdoing. I am grateful I can fill that role because I think it does benefit the individual and society as a whole, but there is always a cost to me personally. Both people and corporations prefer to hide their wrongdoing and will spend considerable resources and energy to hide it. Revealing wrongdoing always releases that energy, and the whistleblower always takes some of the force of that explosion. Whistleblowing is the correct behavior, but it is costly.

Look for a chance to be called an advocate

A person who stands up for someone that cannot stand for themselves is an advocate. We have all had advocates. These people saw that we were in need and could not help ourselves. Rather than giving us a resource, they went to authorities on our behalf to secure aid. For example, when I was struggling with math in 3rd grade, my parents talked to the teacher about options for extra help in math. They advocated for me. They shared with the authority (the teacher) that I was struggling, and the teacher responded by bringing her teacherly resources to the rescue to help me with math.

You will likely benefit from advocates in the workplace. These people may see you struggling and will talk to a person in charge to get you help. The role of an advocate is a significant role to fill, and people should aspire to fill it. I think the role of an advocate is even better than that of an expert because advocates are more valuable than experts. There is a limit to everyone's expertise, so finding an appropriate expert, rather than trying to fix everyone's problems yourself, is a virtue. Advocacy only requires ability in one area: finding experts. In the workplace, this is pretty easy. The "expert" for most situations is the person's direct superior. Human Resources can also be considered professional advocates.

Too often, people see problems and try to solve them when they should be taking on the role of advocate. Instead, we should aspire to help people by connecting them to appropriate resources as much as possible. If it is not an explicit statement in your job description to advocate for people, you should be strategic about how to do this. For instance, Human Resources is an advocacy job. They are trained on how to advocate for co-workers. If you see an opportunity to advocate for a co-worker, the right thing to do would likely be to talk with someone in Human Resources. If that is not an option, it would probably be wise to seek counsel before advocating. A straightforward way is to talk to your supervisor and explain the potential advocacy situation with limited "identifying information" so that the person you're trying to advocate for is not easily identifiable by your description. With enough information supervisors are sometimes compelled to step in whether you want them to or not. This is why you would limit your identifying information to the minimum necessary to make your point. You may see a problem where you need to support a co-worker, but the situation is none of your business, and you should stay out of it. Advocacy is a skill.

What is Office Drama?

Office Drama is broadly described as statements or discussions about people who work in your office that have nothing to do with work happening in the office. Gossips intend for the discussion to be intensely critical. Office drama has two qualities that appear to be opposed. First, office drama has the quality of being distracting from work. Many people will complain that office meetings are an inefficient and poor use of time because people discuss too many things that do not directly apply to the job. When co-workers talk poorly about each other, they can focus less on the work product and more on the character or personality of the worker. Most decisions made in the office result from organizational needs, a summary of facts, or a financial or other "bottom line" issue. Yet, workers can often take it personally or believe that the decision was for the punishment of an individual rather than the company's overall good. These interactions have little to nothing to do with the worker's work, but the intensity or absurdity of the personalization can take away from worker productivity.

The second quality of office drama explains why it still exists in every office setting where two or more people work: it's entertaining. People tolerate and even cause office drama because they like it. Many people can find intense focus on work to be boring. Most people find other people's lives more exciting than their work. Most professionals on the spectrum I talk to are either not aware of office drama or do not like it. I assure you that drama exists everywhere, so if you do not think it helpful, it might be best to ignore it if you can. I believe managing office drama can be tiresome, and ultimately I (and most people I talk to) prefer to find my <u>work</u> engaging, so that office drama is of no interest to me and does not tempt me to get off-task.

There are a couple of qualities of office drama of which to be aware. First, office drama is driven primarily by gossip. Most people gossip occasionally, but gossiping generally becomes less acceptable as one ages. Gossip is incompatible with maturity. Listening to gossip, even without generating gossip, is considered gossiping. I encourage all people to avoid gossip as I find it fundamentally destructive to relationships and reputations, including the reputation of the gossiping person. Even though almost everyone finds office drama entertaining on some level, people can develop an intolerance for it, especially those who are more committed to their jobs and in positions of authority. Finally, engaging in or perpetuating office drama is challenging to do safely. It requires considerable effort and time and a somewhat innate sense of people's appreciation for or tolerance of office drama. To that end, I don't recommend engaging in office drama. It is hard to do well, and the stakes are high as management usually sees office drama as getting in the way of productivity.

With that said, office drama appears to be the staple of all office settings. Therefore, it is good to be aware of it to avoid it, so that the risks of engagement are mitigated.

Office Romance

Office romance is the initiation of a romantic (sexual or non-sexual) relationship with a co-worker. Before they are your romantic partner, the person must be a co-worker to qualify as an office romance. Office romances often must be officially announced to management, especially if they are ongoing. This rule exists because romance complicates pre-existing relationships and almost always becomes the primary way two people relate. Co-workers may have interacted exclusively as co-workers, meaning they interacted when they were in the same space for work purposes, and if not for work, they did not interact. The purpose of interaction was usually to accomplish a work task, even if that was chatting during a holiday party. They would not be talking at a holiday party if they did not first work together.

Adding a romantic element to the co-worker relationship means that people no longer interact only for work. They now voluntarily interact additionally and primarily to build their relationship. They do so because they are interested in knowing each other outside of work-related activities. This interest can create incredible tension when people should be interacting for work-related reasons (because they're at work) instead of interacting for any other reason. Of course, you should be working when you're at work, but office romance can intrude on this focus.

Some people say you should never have a romantic relationship with a co-worker. Some say that romance always takes precedent over every other relationship (including co-workers). Some people choose to create a co-worker relationship with a romantic partner, and some warn against that. Some always mix romance with work, and some never combine romance with work. The guidelines for how one manages co-worker and romantic partner relationships are not clear, so I can make no definitive rule of thumb for these situations. All people, however, should be respectful of the disruption a romantic interaction can have with co-workers. It is not a superficial or meaningless thing to initiate romantic contact with a co-worker. Nor is it always good to become your spouse or romantic partner's co-worker. You should approach each situation with extreme care and thoughtfulness.

You might be asking why co-workers even have romantic interactions. Such relationships happen for the same reason most romantic interactions happen: drive and opportunity. Co-workers spend a lot of time around each other, learn progressively more about each other over time, and are generally in the same phase of life. Drive increases, barriers decrease, and opportunity increases over time. You will likely see an office romance during the time you are working as a professional. Probably more than one.

What is my reputation?

Workers should be interested in their reputation. Specifically, they should be interested in how their co-workers (peers) think of them and how people in authority think of them.

Even though the work product plays a more significant role in deciding what you do all day, preference can still influence how the product is achieved. In school, teachers would tell you to pick partners or assign captains to pick teams. Preference mattered a great deal in group activities because teachers would often build it into the process of selecting groups. In school, one's reputation was a big deal because someone could pick you for a group that made your work more fun, interesting, or easier; or you could be chosen for a group that was the opposite. Worse, you could remain unpicked or get assigned to groups with the other non-preferred kids.

There is a stronger focus on the product in the work world, but companies expect workers to make some decisions about things that affect the bottom line. For instance, in school, the point was to learn how to work in a group. To that end, some teachers might assign groups to pair people with low preference with those with high preference. This decision was supposed to make each person learn something from the other to work better in groups. Since the product is the goal of group work at work, people with low preference will be eliminated from groups or otherwise penalized for having a low preference. Low preference at work is seen as a liability because people don't want to work with you, which affects the product.

Because of this, if you are a person with a bad reputation and have a low preference, you are more in danger of being marginalized or fired. It matters what your reputation is. Co-workers will complain about you; your boss will have to figure out what to do with someone no one wants to work with.

Others see people who have positive reputations at work or high preference as friendly, kind, pleasant, hardworking, reasonable, funny, focused, problem-solvers, outgoing, confident, or competent. Notice that competence is only one of many qualities that promote a positive reputation. It is certainly possible to have any one of these qualities and still have a low preference, including the quality of competence. If a person is competent but hostile, no one will want to work with them. Some qualities, like niceness, are stronger predictors of preference. I have met plenty of people who are the best at what they do at work but are so unkind that no one wants to work with them. Competence is necessary, but being unkind creates an incredible liability for even the most competent workers.

How does one evaluate their reputation? I think it's safe to say that you probably don't know what other people think of you unless they tell you. My ability to guess my reputation, even as a psychologist, is still minimal. I distinctly remember sitting in a team-building activity in a staff meeting. The person leading the training described four different personalities and instructed everyone to get into groups based on these types. The types were distinct and straightforward, but I remember thinking that I could give instances where I acted like any of the four types. I was stuck, so I asked the person next to me which group I should join. They looked at me like I had said a joke and then hesitatingly told me which group I should join.

This entirely true story says a couple of things. First, we can meaningfully differentiate various types of people and workers. Second, it's not just "good and bad" workers, but the groupings are more complex. For instance, I mentioned several different qualities of highly preferred people and, even to some extent, described the relative value of those qualities. Someone might describe you as good or bad, but it is also more complicated than that. Third, when I think about my reputation, I usually start with what I want it to be and then deductively come up with examples to prove my case. This process is highly subjective and leads to inaccuracies. You want to know what people think about you, not have your suspicions confirmed. Fourth, people generally don't know what their reputation is and also don't know that they don't know. This confusion explained why my co-worker thought I was making a joke. The answer was so obvious that she couldn't believe my question was serious. Fifth, most people think you know what they think of you. This assumption couldn't be further from the truth since, as a society, we are generally more polite than honest. This tendency is where the term "white lie" comes from and the justification that a lie can be a good thing. It's also why truth-telling is often called "being blunt," and people who tell the truth are called "jerks."

You will have to ask people directly to tell you your reputation. Then, you will probably have to convince them that you don't know what it is and do want to know. Finally, you will have to disarm their instinct to intentionally withhold negative information from you. For instance, you will have to encourage them to be "totally honest" and even talk about the negative parts of your reputation. Then, you should thank them for being honest, especially about the negative aspects, since it is challenging for most people to criticize others to their face (rather than gossiping behind their backs).

I would recommend starting this process with your boss instead of a co-worker. Many people I talk to say they prefer asking a friend at work but don't realize that the people they think of as friends are not their friends. It is not uncommon to think someone likes you when they just tolerate you. This situation is an example of not knowing, or even being able to see, one's reputation without being told.

Chapter 6

Supervisors

Everyone has a boss, and they go by many names. Some of the most popular titles are manager and supervisor. As stated previously, most businesses are organized hierarchically. Whether your company has two or dozens of levels, this chapter is devoted mainly to your relationship with the person one level up from you.

Why your manager might be bad at their job

It makes sense to address the belief or experience that seems to cause the most consternation to my clients. Your manager is not necessarily in their position of authority because they are especially good at being a manager. The Peter Principle (i.e., "people in a hierarchy tend to rise to their 'maximum level of incompetence.'") sheds some light on why your manager might dislike their job, be ineffective, or not know as much about your job as you do.

When people do outstanding work, they are commonly rewarded in two ways. Usually, employers pay them more. However, compensation is not always in the form of increased pay. Instead, employers can reward outstanding employees with better benefits or work conditions (e.g., closer parking space, larger office, new scrub brush, etc.). The other and possibly more common way people are rewarded with good work is advancement. American work culture has a common myth about "starting in the mailroom and working your way up." A couple of prominent stories support this myth, but the point is that work culture believes that the average person should want to have increased status at any job. In reality, increased status means more responsibility through leadership. Therefore, most people believe that everyone should ultimately want to be in charge.

The reality of this reward method hits most people when they spend more time managing people than they are doing the actual work for which they trained. I have talked with many people in the tech industry, especially those who went from working on the development of cutting edge technology to managing the people working on the development of cutting edge technology. They didn't want to manage people, per se; they were just being rewarded for their outstanding work with cutting-edge technology. But at some point, working your way up usually means getting into the management of people. It is not uncommon to find managers with impressive technical skills that don't use those skills for their job. Instead, they manage people who use those skills, but the managers may have no actual training in managing people. People-management is a skill in itself.

In the same way someone is told to cut down a tree but not how to use a chainsaw, many managers are assigned to run departments or teams, but not taught how to manage people. As a result, while they are poorly managing people, their original skillsets are becoming more and more obsolete. This process is one way you may get a manager who seems terrible at their job.

Most managers I talk to say that the management of people is the worst part of their job. This observation is both sad and understandable since most managers had no intention of being people-managers, to begin with. But unfortunately, dissatisfaction and incompetence are often passed down to workers who say the worst part of their job is their manager.

What does a good manager do?

Over the years, I have had many bosses, supervisors, and managers and have participated in many worker/supervisor relationships. Some have been excellent, and some have been terrible. Most have been ok or forgettable. The worst bosses made it clear that managing me was the worst part of their job. They expressed dislike of me, dissatisfaction with me, or have simply been unavailable-as if the only reason they exist (i.e., to manage me) was not an actual part of their job.

The best manager I had said something like this to me: "My primary job is to make you good at your job." This statement sums up a manager's job and should be the standard by which all managers are judged. A warning, though: I have only heard or experienced such management like this a few times in my life, and there was only one person I can recall who came out and described that as the foundation of our relationship. With that said, I think most people in management want to like their job and want their workers to be successful. Some of them need encouragement, though. A few you meet will simply need to exit management and return to being a worker. After decades of working for people and generally being regarded as a competent employee, I now work in a situation where I choose not to have a boss or employees.

A good manager focuses primarily on the success of the worker. It is true that the manager has a "big picture" view of the group's work and probably has information the worker does not have on the significance of his work. Good managers can say "no" to ideas that seem to make sense at the moment and immediately increase productivity. This seemingly inexplicable choice often happens because the managers are looking at the group's needs (including those of the business) when considering the suggestions of the individual worker. Good managers are approachable and take the time to listen and understand what is going on with their workers. Good managers are excellent communicators but also ask a lot of questions. Good managers let workers make choices with the understanding that they, the manager, are ultimately responsible for the work of their subordinates. Good managers maintain a clever balance of approachability and authority with their workers. Good managers prefer being respected over being liked. It is important to note that good managers exist and do good work, even if they have a difficult day. You will find no end to the people with gripes and complaints about their boss, and I encourage the average worker to avoid getting involved in complaining about such things. If you decide that your manager is not meeting some basic standards of competence for management, it's best in many cases to look for a new job than to complain or lament your situation. See below to understand why.

The final note I want to bring on this issue is that most people who complain to me about their bosses tend to complain outside their level of competence or understanding. By this, I mean they criticize their boss for behaviors or decisions the boss makes when they do not or cannot know how their boss came to that decision. My favorite story on this issue is one where I led a support group of young workers with disabilities, and we talked about bad managers we had known. One person told the story about being fired because he "found an efficiency" in his work that made his boss look bad. Out of spite and embarrassment, he said, his boss fired him. He concluded that his boss was so stupid and resentful. I asked a couple more questions about the incident, and this group member said he started delegating some of the work he found boring to a co-worker who didn't seem to mind the task. He had no idea how wrong his behavior was. It turns out he was fired justly, and for a behavior everyone knows is wrong (i.e., you cannot assign tasks to your co-workers, only managers can do that). He had focused on the idiocy of his boss at the expense of understanding how his own behavior was inappropriate.

What does it mean to "go over the boss's head"?

What happens when your manager is so bad that you feel the treatment you receive is unjust, immoral, or otherwise gets in the way of your success? One option is to talk to your boss's boss about it. There is almost always one level up in your organization. If your boss is the CEO of the company, most companies have a Board of Directors that act as the boss of the CEO. This authority structure is all over the US, especially in the government. The point of this is that no one should be above criticism. Even the President of the United States must answer to the voters.

The reality of this authority structure does not always work out the way we think it should. Movies and TV shows love the trope of the worker working under unjust conditions for an evil boss and going over the boss's head to exact justice. Even though this is an option for most workers, I do not recommend it. As stated above, and if it's an option, I recommend getting another job before going over the boss's head. The reason for this is that in addition to facilitating the worker's work, the manager must maintain the status and stability of management. Your manager's manager's job is to make your manager successful. When complaining to the boss's boss, you're complaining about that person's work. Your manager may be so bad at their job that they will get corrected or fired and something positive will happen to you, like get a new, more competent boss. More likely, the higher-ups will discover that your manager is adequate for their job and will direct scrutiny on you. "Why are you complaining? Do you like causing trouble? Let's see about your job performance." You just criticized someone's competence to their face, so there is some context for scrutiny. This is somewhat like the situation a whistleblower may find himself facing.

So you find yourself in a situation where working for your boss is difficult and untenable. You have a couple of options.

1. You can talk to your boss. Most bosses are bad at their job because they never set out to manage people. They may have accepted a promotion and initially saw it as evidence that they were doing good work but later found out that they didn't like the reality of leadership. Self-advocacy to the boss is a great first option. Focus on the challenges you are having and avoid any commentary on your boss's competence. For example, rather than, "you're assigning me too much work," you can say,

"I'm having trouble keeping up with the workload." Or, "you don't give me enough support," can be turned into, "I need more support." Give your boss a chance to manage.

2. You can talk to Human Resources (HR). People in HR have the training to manage people. They also have some level of immunity from the machinations of management.

3. You can start looking for a new job right away. I think this is a good thing to do regularly anyway. More on this later.

4. You can ask for direct feedback on your work. Many managers I talk to dislike giving their workers formal feedback. To this end, many simply do not provide their workers feedback, even when it could make things better for everyone. Hating your manager might mean you need some feedback on how to do your work. You might be doing a poor job, and instead of correcting you, your boss simply chooses to let you flop around. I have had plenty of managers who seem to let me flounder in my job. They were holding off on telling me how to do better because they didn't want me to get mad at them all the while. This perspective is a naïve one for a manager, but it happens more often than we think.

5. Go over the boss's head. If you have exhausted all other avenues and feel that this is the only option, go for it. I would not go here first since this will likely cause you some hardship, even if it is the just thing to do and solves the original problem. You should approach this issue with respect and gravity and should have actual evidence to support your complaints.

A final note on this topic: you can never go wrong seeking good counsel. If you find yourself in a challenging situation at work, you should have someone in your life you can consult, like a spouse, parent, or friend. Many of the conditions people encounter at work are complicated, and people generally may not know precisely how to handle all of them. Nevertheless, we all, myself included, have people to consult and ask for advice and perspective. If you only have one non-work relationship, make it someone who can advise you.

The cost of laziness

A standard piece of advice and a vital tool for any worker's skill set is to ask for additional work when you finish what is assigned. This advice is especially relevant in low-level jobs where the assigned work is sometimes insufficient to fill one's workday. Salaried people and people who work in higher-skilled jobs don't usually have as much trouble staying busy. Often the opposite is the case-they must work to balance their time as there is always more they could be doing.

How workers spend their time is not based exclusively on what work there is to do. Often it is also based on one's approach to work. I have had many teenagers in my office tell me the job they are looking for is one where they can do as little work as possible. "Pay me not to work? How can I pass that up?" Often, people look for jobs that seem to have a lot of sitting around involved. The problem is that even if your job offers you the opportunity to "get paid to do nothing," that is rarely acceptable. The expectation when one is at work is that they are working. The people you see at the department store or collecting your garbage, but are looking at their phones or otherwise appear to be relaxing, are doing it wrong. That behavior harms their reputation at work, and it is much easier for them to get fired for minor things or to have their hours reduced. You should be very careful about having a reputation for relaxation or break-taking at work, even if you feel like you are getting away with it. "My boss saw me on my phone and didn't say anything," is what I hear a lot. They conclude that it must be ok to be on their phone. Nothing could be further from the truth. This person should assume that the boss recorded their off-task behavior and didn't correct them because everyone knows not to be off task. Such behaviors should not require direct correction, even if it is helpful.

In all jobs, from the lowliest fry cook at a fast-food restaurant to the most powerful CEO, people come to work to work. If you get breaks during the day, take them discretely in the break room. The other thing to consider is that even if you are a slacker at work, there is likely someone with your same job who is a hard worker. Employers are comparing you to that hard-working person; that hard worker sets the standard of behavior. People make fun of "teacher's pets" in school, but such people can get more pay and promotions in the work world. Use whatever excuse you might for justifying why this person got more pay and more hours than you (e.g., I don't want to work here more than I already am, I hate this place), but the fact is that laziness is out of place and thus poorly tolerated in the work world.

The cost of success

Believe it or not, there is some cost to doing a great job. I will list out some of these costs and explain them a bit. I want to be clear, though, that it is a virtue and always recommended that you do the best you can in all situations at work. A strong work ethic and having the reputation of being a "good worker" can make up for almost any shortcoming a person has at work. Be that as it may, there are some potential costs as well. In no particular order, here are some costs I have seen exacted on workers who are known as hard workers.

1. I've already mentioned that good work leads to promotions. I won't go into this again, but the downside of doing good work is that people often want to replicate your good worker status by putting you in charge of other workers and often incompetent workers (who are not getting promoted). They think, and they are usually correct, that you being in charge makes it more likely that the job given to a team will get done.

2. People who work hard and ask for more work tend to get more work. Bosses give hard workers more work than lazy workers. It's unfair, but that's how the world works. Again, if you're the lazy worker and are given less and less work (because it's reassigned to the hard worker), you will eventually be worked out of a job. But increasing amounts of assignments for the hard worker are a reality. It's a cumulative process, and the only way I have ever heard that this process was reversed is through self-advocacy.

3. Hard workers tend to gain a negative reputation among lazy workers. It's the same concept of being criticized for being smart or getting good grades. Lazy people paradoxically criticize successful people for being successful. It makes sense because they are being negatively evaluated based on your hard work, but they could step it up and avoid that criticism. Being criticized for doing one's job at work doesn't feel affirming for sure, but it is one of the realities of the work world.

Workers seem to fit very nicely into a bell curve. There are people at the extremes, for sure-terrible workers and exceptional workers, but most workers find themselves somewhere in the middle. I have found being a middle-type worker to be the most pleasant and predictable situation. Highly competent people are constantly assigned more work, and highly incompetent people are often being fired. Both extremes seem to struggle with maintaining a balanced life. I should note, however, that as I have progressed in my experience and skill, I meet fewer and fewer incompetent workers and more and more highly competent workers. If you plan to get better at your vocation over time, expect to be surrounded by more highly talented people.

Should I accept the promotion?

Before I respond to this question, the reader should know my bias. I don't understand some people's impulse to lead. I couldn't care less about being a leader. Yet, as a white, professional, adult male, I often get asked to be in charge of things. I have way more leadership experience than an equally qualified woman or a person of color. With that said, I know people that were made to be in leadership positions. It's something they want to do, not just for the recognition or authority, but because they are good at it.

A person offered a promotion should be clear about the nature of the additional responsibility that comes along with the promotion. No promotion exists with the same or less responsibility as the job you currently hold. The best way to find out the details of the increased responsibility is to ask directly what the promotion will entail as far as increased expectations. For instance, I was once asked to serve on a Board of Trustees for an organization, and I asked directly how often the Board meets and when they meet. Then I asked about how many events Board members must attend at the organization and how often the Board communicates between meetings. This information helped me make a more informed choice about the offer. In another case, I was offered a promotion in a job and was told there would be more work and pay to compensate for the additional time. In addition, there would be more meetings that would include managing people below me and reporting to people above me. Again, the details were laid out in the contract, and I was able to discuss their practicalities with the person offering the promotion, which helped me make an informed decision.

Promotions almost always require more time spent in meetings. If you dislike meetings, reconsider the promotion. Promotions also usually mean less time doing tasks you like, especially using your technical skillset. As people advance, their time at work tends to increase while so-called free time tends to decrease. As a result, people report the balance between work and non-work tends to be harder to manage.

On the other hand, promotions also mean more money and more recognition. Many people, once promoted, report feeling more control over the product and that the work they do has a more significant impact on the company. Some people discover that they like leadership and management and are good at it. But, again, our school system doesn't systematically train people to be leaders, so some people do not know they like leadership and have not practiced their leadership skills until a promotion forces them to lead.

Should you accept the promotion? First, be as clear as you can about what the promotion means for how your job and life will change. Next, be careful about looking at and overemphasizing a single aspect of the promotion (like more money) in making your decision. Finally, seek counsel and get another person's perspective on it, even if you do not follow their advice.

Why you should update your resume and apply for jobs annually

Years ago, a friend shared with me that he applied for jobs annually. What was interesting about this habit is we were working together, and he seemed to like his job. I thought people only applied for jobs when they had to, but this was not the case. He had several excellent reasons for his ritual that I want to share with you.

1. Applying for jobs meant he had to update his resume and online work profile yearly. This habit is helpful because people who go years between updating their resume find the task overwhelming when it finally comes time to update it. It usually takes me about five minutes to update my resume if I do it at least annually. The information is accurate (and I don't have to look at an old calendar to figure out when things probably happened), and if I see an opportunity to ask

someone for a general letter of recommendation, I can do it promptly.

2. Scanning job postings annually caused him to evaluate the relevance of his skills. He often found that posts for jobs similar to his own required additional skills or certifications. Most industries advance and mature, and a person's skills and competencies should advance similarly. There's nothing worse than a physician working from out-of-date research or a teacher who doesn't know how to use modern technology. He would also use his findings to make a case that his current workplace should finance his continuing education. This request did not always meet with agreement, but sometimes it did.

3. Sometimes my friend would get interviews for jobs, and he would be forced to work on his interview skills. This practice kept those skills sharp and up to date and helped him do his job more effectively because he examined his strengths and weaknesses. It was the only time he wore a suit and tie. He would also get a haircut. All workers, especially those in leadership, seem to benefit from some intense scrutiny from time to time. Workers are always at risk for complacency.

4. My friend noted salaries and benefits in these job postings and used this information when he was negotiating his current work contract.

5. Finally, my friend would occasionally find better jobs. This outcome was not the ultimate goal of this annual tradition, but it was an occasional benefit. These better jobs would help him in one of two ways. First, and most obviously, he would interview and possibly be offered a better job. If he accepted the better position, he would have a better job. Because he

liked his current job, there was no cost to interviewing for and wanting a job and then being turned down for the job. He still had a job he liked. Consequently, this confidence of not <u>needing</u> a new job helped him relax during the interviews. With more confidence, he did better in the interviews and was subsequently offered many jobs. Second, if an employer offered him the job, he would almost always ask his boss to match the offer. This request might seem manipulative, and it would be if this were a friendship, but this was a work relationship, so this was appropriate.

You may not want to make this an annual ritual like my friend, but it is wise to make job applications a part of your general career development. I look at job postings regularly. Even though I love what I do, I occasionally apply for other jobs. It's good to review my resume and letters of recommendation, look at my training and qualifications, and otherwise contact other people in my field and related fields. I have found, thankfully, that for more than a decade, I have not been able to find a job superior to my own. I like my job, but I am intensely satisfied with my good fortune when I can't find a better one. And my resume is always within 12 months of being up to date, just in case.

Chapter 7

A Good Job

There are many ways to describe what makes a job a good job. Look online, and you will find studies and opinion polls that discuss the best jobs, best places to work, or happiest employees. These are undoubtedly interesting places to start looking at what makes a job suitable. Still, the process is a lot more complicated than examining any single factor.

An examination of your resources and goals will help you move in the direction of finding a good job. However, on many accounts, your options will often be decided by people and systems outside your control. For instance, it used to be more common for people to work for one company for their entire careers. Today it is more common for people to hold many jobs over multiple companies during their careers. As much as you would like to take some time to find the perfect job and then work it for 40 years, that just might not be possible.

Another consideration is a good job will likely change over time. For instance, when I was in high school, landscaping was a good job because it was low skill and low demand on my time, but relatively good pay. Landscaping would not be an excellent job for me right now. My current job is optimal because of its flexibility. My current job would not have been outstanding in high school because I was unqualified.

Following are some factors people find helpful to consider when looking for work. It is important to recall that I am referring to pursuing a good job and not the dream job. I don't think dream jobs exist. All jobs have their upsides and downsides. Since dream jobs are supposed to be all good and not bad, you'll likely never find such a job. On the other hand, good jobs are easy to find. Also, good jobs will change as other factors in your life change. It's pretty normal for a good job to become a not-so-good job and for people to look for better jobs.

Pay

Pay is listed first because people almost always bring it up first. As a variable that predicts happiness in work, pay plateaus in its predictive power. Increased pay only makes a job "better" up to a point. After that point, increased pay doesn't affect job satisfaction as much as other factors. I'm bringing this up because "more" pay is not always better. If you are working for minimum wage, increased pay can improve your job satisfaction for quite a long time. However, if you have been working as a professional for 20 years, you may have reached the point where more money does not increase the quality of the job. Go ahead and look up the current number (in 2021, it's around 70K in the US), but increased pay leads to increased happiness at work up to the point where you can comfortably live a middle-class lifestyle. After that, the ability of increased income to increase your work happiness tends to drop off.

This issue is important because some people want to "make a lot of money" as a primary goal of their job search. However, this goal is problematic for several reasons.

1. There are many low-paying jobs, and the number of jobs that pay more decreases as the pay goes up. So if you want to make "a lot of money" in your career, the volume of jobs you have to choose from will be tiny relative to the total number of jobs.

2. As stated above, making a lot of money does not necessarily mean liking your job more. So, in addition to making a lot of money, you will have to consider other factors that will help you to enjoy your job. Therefore, this step will further limit your pool of possible employment.

3. One main reason jobs pay a lot is because they are hard. A friend earns a lot as a physician, but he also works about twice as many hours as I do. He doesn't usually look happy. He mostly looks tired. In my field, some of the highest paying jobs are working for prisons. That's great for people who like to work in prisons, but that group is also tiny. To bring more people to the job, they increase the pay.

You will likely be happy in a job that pays enough to help you live a reasonable lifestyle. Therefore, it would make sense that you get some sort of an idea of the monthly budget of a middle-class individual and then do the math to figure out how much you need to make to live that way. In this way, you can use pay as a useful variable for finding a good job.

Training

What sort of training are you willing to do? Some jobs require years of training. Some jobs take just an afternoon to learn. Some people are unable or unwilling to complete college. Some people will only attend training for a job they know they will love. I want to be clear that I'm not necessarily saying that the more you're willing to be trained, the more you will like your job. Not at all. I know many highly qualified people who don't even work in the fields they are trained in. I also know people with minimal training that love their jobs. However, it makes sense that the more training you have, the more jobs you can work. A nuclear engineer can work at a fast-food restaurant, but the average fast-food worker is not qualified to be a nuclear engineer. Training usually correlates positively to opportunity.

You might also consider what kind of training you can tolerate. For example, I spent seven years in graduate training. If I had spent all of those seven years sitting in a classroom, I might not have made it (only two were full-time classroom work). On the other hand, some training is entirely "on the job" in the form of an apprenticeship. Some training is general and classical, and some is focused and specific. A classical training experience is similar to what happens in high school. Focused training occurs during the first week of working at McDonald's.

If you cannot imagine going to college and then grad school for seven years, spending days in the classroom and evenings in the library, you should not become a lawyer. Likewise, suppose you cannot imagine your training consisting of carrying heavy hoses up flights of stairs and applying pressure to an open chest wound. In that case, you should not become a firefighter.

Setting

Some people imagine working in an office building, some in a forest. As a teen, I couldn't stand being inside all day for work. While my brother worked in fast food, I was landscaping. Now I work inside and look out the window and take walks. Sit down, stand up, and wear suits or scrubs. Consider your personal preferences for the setting where you will spend most of your waking hours as an adult. Some settings could be dangerous to your health, especially with long-term exposure, like working with known carcinogens or sitting down all day.

The setting is something I might look at changing if I am looking for a better job. For example, I work inside and by myself most days. Could I have everything I love about my job but be outside? This change might make my job a better job. How about doing what I do, but with co-workers? This, too, might be an improvement. These considerations are some of the ways setting affects your search for a better job.

Meaning

More than good pay, people often say they value how meaningful their job is. There are dozens of TV shows and movies about people giving up high-paying jobs for more meaningful employment. This story, however, is a real thing and not just a fairy tale. It is crucial to people that they find their work meaningful. I should note that nearly everyone you talk to will say they want their work to count for something. No one ever says they want to be forgotten when they die and for their work to have had no impact on anyone. Of course, all people want their work to count, but they may not get any enjoyment from their work unless it counts for something and they feel that their work has meaning.

Meaning tends to be easier to find in work in service of others, but I want to note that it is possible to turn even the most selfless and humanitarian-focused job into empty self-worship. For instance, I have met people who work for Food Banks that find the job empty and soul-less, and people in so-called soul-less professions like accounting and finance who are very excited about the opportunity to do good in their careers and help people.

It is also likely that what you find meaningful will change over time as you age and mature. For example, many people working for political campaigns are young. This observation is no anomaly. They get older, have more education, and often become teachers or government workers. Like I said earlier, young people tend to emphasize the importance of being financially well off, and when they get there, they discover it is not as high of a priority as they thought it would be.

Extenuating Circumstances

This final topic wouldn't be necessary except that most children in the West are told they can be who they want to be and do what they want to do without limit. This message is encapsulated in the phrase, "You can have it all." On the one hand, this is an optimistic way to look at an individual's prospects. But, on the other hand, there is nothing even remotely true about this statement. It can be very upsetting for people successfully indoctrinated with this message to discover it is nonsense.

People often have lives that dictate where they work and what they do. Money and family are two significant factors in deciding what jobs a person pursues. People with lots of money tend to have more options, in general, than those with little money. People tied to their family (emotionally, financially, functionally) or town look for opportunities that allow them to stay close to where they grew up. Some people see extenuating circumstances as limitations for job opportunities, and I think this is reasonable. However, it is also legitimate to look at these circumstances as natural ways to cull the field of job options. People who had opportunities they chose not to take, for one reason or another, seem to be those dealing with the most doubt and regret when it comes to jobs. Extenuating circumstances can limit opportunity but don't seem to increase the regret or doubt in the same way.

There are many other things to consider when looking for a job, but these are some of the significant considerations. You should look at those factors that will help you (or cause you) to limit the field of potential jobs. Despite what you might have been told, more options are not always better. Too many options can make any choice you make dissatisfying. As much as we live in a "more is better" culture, you will benefit from choosing from a modest list: not too many, not too few. This modest list will make it easier for the job you choose to be a good job.

A good job is one you can be satisfied with, and not necessarily the one that stands out from all the other bad jobs. This approach will also mean that even so-called bad jobs can become good jobs. Working as a landscaper was an excellent job for me at one time, but now it would not be as good (even if there were parts that I enjoyed). My future good job could be one I now consider a lousy job. In grad school, I trained to be a researcher and thought being a clinician was the worst of the options I had. Looking back on it, following opportunities and being clear about my goals served me well.

Bad Jobs

It makes sense to say a word about bad jobs. There are some jobs out there that are obviously bad. Jobs that require someone to break the law or involve blatant abuse and injustice are bad jobs. One can easily differentiate these from good jobs. These are not the jobs I'm talking about here. People don't usually need help sorting out those jobs.

The kind of bad jobs I'm talking about are those that are subtly bad. They have some negative qualities, but they have some positive attributes too. Bad jobs can also be jobs that are not bad for everyone but are certainly a bad fit for you, for one reason or another.

Poor leadership can make any job a lousy job. It can be the case that you loved your job, and then you got a new boss (or lost a great boss) that does not lead properly, and all of a sudden, your job feels unworkable. This scenario is not only a message to leaders to do good work, but to you, the worker who might someday have a position of influence and authority. How one leads makes a considerable difference to those they are leading.

Consider, for a moment, jobs where all the workers are young and no one has much tenure. By that, I mean that few or no people have worked there for a long time. Bad jobs tend to have high turnover. I see this a lot in my field. Some jobs require people to be trained at a high level for clinical work but are staffed by those who have minimal training and receive minimal support on the job. In this case, the company needs "bodies" to meet specific quotas more than minds to get work done. I imagine these workers like chunks of wood thrown into the fire that are quickly consumed and need to be replaced by another piece of wood. If one approaches this job not as a career but as an opportunity to gain experience for a better job, they can turn into good jobs. Mostly though, what makes them suitable is that they are temporary. Once you've learned what you can know, you move on.

Bad jobs are not necessarily those that lack excitement or are boring and monotonous. I have talked with people who chose positions because they were boring. They reported that they wanted to save their mental energy for pursuits outside work. They appreciated that their tedious job paid the bills and required little mental energy, but not because they were lazy. On the other hand, all exciting things become routine over time. For example, people who travel for a living eventually get tired of sleeping in hotels and spending time at airports. So again, it's not the nature of the job but how the job works for you that matters.

Bad jobs are often made that way, when they are made bad, by the workplace itself. Consequently, a person should be cautious about a job that seems too good to be true or trying hard to sell itself to workers. These can be jobs that seem to pay more than you would expect, have benefits (e.g., work from home, company car) that are uncommon, or are overly excited to have you work there. Such may be OK for some, but the worker needs to get clarity about the nature of the work. For example, I talked to one person who made a lot of money at his job but worked so many hours that it was not as much money as it seemed per hour and restricted many other enjoyable activities outside of work. I asked him why he was still in the job since it appeared to be so stressful and sacrificial (and not in a good way), and he said, "This is the life I have chosen." The job was consistent with how he wanted to live his life. It was an excellent job at that time, but once he decided he no longer wanted to live that life, it would be a lousy job, and he would need to get out.

Multiple jobs in multiple fields

The modern worker tends to have more jobs throughout their career than previous generations. This change seems like a normal fluctuation in society, and this trend may shift again in the future. It is worth mentioning that you might have jobs in multiple fields over your lifetime. There will likely be a discernable thread to your job choices.

Still, openness to working across fields or disciplines in your career (or careers) will increase the chances of finding good jobs, especially those that reflect your goals and needs. Cross-field careers are possible for a couple of reasons.

First, people just seem to stay in jobs for less time, in general, than they used to. Moving from one position to the next always allows moving between fields or disciplines. Second, people's training seems to be more multi-disciplinary. I recall lecturing on "the death of the liberal arts education" about ten years ago, but I am aware of no such demise. There aren't even signs of such. I was way off, and the audience, made up of liberal arts educators, was right to boo me (which they did). The liberal arts education is considered a broad and well-rounded education. It was also called the Classical Education, which focused on general learning across all major disciplines. This attitude toward education remains dominant as colleges and universities try to make their graduates as marketable as possible in the work world. Even my education, which is extremely specific, still qualifies me for cross-disciplinary jobs from teaching to research to administration. Even clergy have degrees similar to mine. Finally, the areas where jobs seem to be increasing and growing have a more collaborative and multi-disciplinary approach, like medicine and tech. Even though specialization in these fields is also increasing, the "triage" (e.g., teams in various job sectors formed of professionals from multiple disciplines) method is also growing. For these and other reasons, I think it's wise to be open to the notion that you might work in more than one field over your career, and not just more than one job.

Lateral Moves

A final note is that a good job is more likely to result from a lateral move. A lateral move is across the hierarchy, not up or down the hierarchy. The work world seems committed to the notion that people constantly need to move "up" in their careers. More money, more status. This mentality appears to be driven more by the company's needs than the worker's needs, so it's right to be skeptical of offers of such vertical moves.

Previously, I talked about what things can turn a good job into a bad one, and most of them were structural changes in the company, like losing a good boss. Becoming the boss is not usually the answer to the problem of losing a good boss. Getting another good boss would be a more appropriate solution. Better yet, finding another good boss to work for makes sense. This switch is a lateral move: same pay and status, new and better boss.

Lateral moves can be within or between companies. Some companies, like Salesforce, are famous for their ability to move people laterally within the company. One reason Salesforce can do this is that they are a huge company. Smaller companies might not have as many opportunities for such moves, so that the right decision may be a lateral move to another company.

To most of my clients, the idea of a lateral move makes sense. If the problem with your job is your boss (or some other aspect of the company culture), get a new boss (or a new company). To many of my clients, it makes no sense to solve a work culture issue by seeking promotion or more pay. This solution is not apparent to most people, so I state it here. Also, as I said above, it's not usually the first choice of the company because the easiest and most obvious thing for a company to do with an unhappy employee is to give them more responsibility. Therefore, the vertical move might be right for you but make such a move only after you have considered the lateral move.

Chapter 8

Self Employed

Self-employment is on the rise in the United States and elsewhere. Some experts point to the 2020 pandemic and the restrictions and limitations the pandemic imposed as a reason. Self-employment was on the increase before that, however. Regardless of the reasons for the increase, you likely know people or have heard of self-employed people. Maybe what they have described to you sounds ideal.

Why you should work for yourself

Self-employment sounds ideal to many people, and there are many reasons to look at this option. Let's examine a few.

There are a lot of social rules for interacting with people in a hierarchical system, such as your boss. Navigating this relationship is not only tricky, but the stakes are high. Specifically, if you get something wrong in your navigation of the relationship, you can be fired. Not getting fired in such a situation can almost be worse because now you have a boss who does not like you. People can get stuck in these terrible hierarchical interactions and relationships, which seems to be a primary contributor to dissatisfaction at work. If you are self-employed, that usually means you are the boss, and you are at the top of the hierarchy (if there even is one).

Interacting with co-workers is an equally intense task with many esoteric and seemingly meaningless rules to help the relationship run smoothly. However, you can do everything technically correct and still end up in an uncomfortable or difficult interaction. The reason for this is that the rules governing social situations are somewhat dynamic, and even if you do them correctly, the other person might not be as astute in the interactions as you. Therefore, even though they break the rules, you can still suffer. Such problematic social interactions are so common (with both bosses and co-workers) that they created a whole department called Human Relations (HR) tasked with dealing with such issues. Being self-employed usually means no co-workers.

The work world has certain traditions that range from quaint to obnoxious. For example, celebrating birthdays in the office is quaint. Usually, there is the tradition of wishing the person a happy birthday in exchange for getting a piece of cake. Staff meetings are, in my opinion, an example of an office tradition that often borders on the obnoxious. Not all office traditions are useless or pointless, but it is easy to turn traditions and routines into frustrating events. I recall the first weeks of moving from working in an office to being self-employed. On Wednesdays at 4 pm, I would marvel that I no longer had to attend a staff meeting (because there was no staff to meet with). No meeting was necessary. Those who are self-employed have much more control over the activities of work that are indirectly related to productivity, such as staff meetings and staff holiday parties. As a result, the productivity-to-time ratio favors productivity for the self-employed rather than working in an office with others.

The self-employed have more control over "soft skill" requirements, such as being on time for work and grooming. If you are not a morning person, starting a business that doesn't require you to be at work before lunch is possible. If you are hypersensitive to noise or light, you can manage that more effectively in a self-employed situation. I have talked with people who would love to do their job from bed. While I do not recommend such a set-up, that is possible for those in a self-employment situation. Control over the work and the work environment is one of the primary reasons people choose self-employment.

Many people I work with have good ideas. I just read an article the other day that says that people quit their jobs because they are not allowed to share feedback up the chain of command or feel ignored when they give feedback. Perhaps you work in a field but not on a product you love. Or, you have an idea about your product, and no one will listen. Self-employment is an excellent option for such people. Greater control over what you do and how you do it is why many people become self-employed.

In 2009 Tim Ferris published his book, *The Four Hour Work Week*. Since that time, people have been questioning many work traditions such as the 40-hour workweek, the cubicle (the small box with fake walls that is large enough to fit a desk and filing cabinet), and even sitting at a desk (i.e., standing desks and treadmills under desks). Self-employment allows a person to adjust some or all of these traditional structures or even double down on others. Some self-employed rent an office in an office building, and some work in cafes and coffee shops. I have talked with some people who bought an RV and did their "desk job" remotely while traveling the country. The point is that with self-employment, you have the control that allows you to work fewer hours or more hours, from home or on the road, wearing a shirt and tie, or just a t-shirt. This freedom to imagine how else your work life might be is enticing to many who choose self-employment.

Hopefully, I have done a reasonable job making self-employment look desirable. However, the question you should ask yourself is, if self-employment is so amazing, why are so many people still working in office buildings or waking up at 6 am and putting on uniforms?

Why you shouldn't work for yourself

According to the World Bank, in 2019, about 7% of workers were self-employed in the United States. In the UK it was 19.5% and 20.3% in Australia. When you look at the numbers in other countries, you will notice that the US has one of the lowest self-employment rates. I think it's fair to say that in the US, being self-employed is hard, and being employed by a business is, by comparison, much more manageable. This finding is because conditions in the US favor employment through companies. Also, the US has the business infrastructure to accommodate the vast majority of workers. These resources may not be accurate for Afghanistan, which had a 79.7% self-employment rate in 2019.

It seems more challenging to be self-employed in the US than in other parts of the world. However, before moving to another country, there are more reasons to reconsider self-employment.

Many people struggle with the transition from high school to college. One of the significant changes is that nobody cares if you go to class or do your work in college. This change is the biggest difference in transitioning from a compulsory environment like high school to a voluntary environment like college (see chapter 2). I have talked with many people who attended college for a couple of months only to discover that they were failing their classes at the end of week 10, and the semester was a complete waste. The reality of college is that you are assigned all of your work on the first day of class, and you take a final exam or complete a project to submit on the last day of class. What happens between day one and the final day is primarily up to you. This work format is also that of self-employment. On the one hand, no one nags you to come to work or do any work. You work when you want, and if you want to do something else, you can do that, and no one cares. As ideal as this sounds, most adults know this can be a recipe for failure and destruction. Most adults who are successful in college, or even adulthood, understand that they must do things they do not want to do. Adults have to get up in the morning, pay bills, clean the toilet, and a whole bunch of other tasks that, all things being equal, they would rather not do. Being self-employed and successful means you not only set goals and expectations for yourself, but you enforce those expectations on yourself. Self-employment requires a considerable level of self-discipline. The self-employed cannot depend on the fear of getting fired to get them out of bed in the morning. I would suggest that if you have not mastered getting out of bed in the morning by the time you start your business, the business is doomed.

Part of the reason the self-employment rate in the US is so low could be because many people lack the self-discipline to be self-employed.

Perhaps you have an idea that is great for a new business. Maybe you have a specialized and highly sought-after skill set that people cannot wait to hire. These are usually the building blocks of a small business that would allow you to be self-employed. Unfortunately, you may lack much of the other 98% of skills needed to make your self-employment situation sustainable. Indeed, self-employed people do not need an HR department since there are no employees to manage. All businesses require considerable expertise to run, however. The self-employed must become experts in finance, banking, marketing, advertising, information technology, web design, and licensing. These are just a few of the demands I have encountered. Perhaps you tell yourself that you will be making so much money that you will just contract people to do everything you don't like. However, you must know enough about those areas not to be taken advantage of or know what to expect from your contractors. The self-employed must have basic knowledge and experience in all of these areas and more. If you have a singular skill set and no desire to learn how to run a business, you should not seek self-employment.

Time management is a struggle for most of my clients on the spectrum and with related neurocognitive disorders. I recall asking a group of students in my social skills class how long it takes to use the bathroom on average. This question references a mundane, daily task and the whole group struggled to come up with an answer. The answer for me is three minutes, and this includes adequate hand-washing. The point is not about spending too long in the bathroom. It's about knowing how long things should take. The self-employed have dozens of tasks, from highly specific like writing an email to a client, to highly general, like taking a lunch break, which all must be considered and fit into a day. Do you lose track of time? Do you get lost in specific enjoyable tasks and find that a lot of time has passed? You should reconsider being self-employed. Many people depend on bells to know when class is over. People unknowingly depend on seeing other people eat to know when to eat. Many people rely on noticing they are alone in the office and it's dark outside to know it is time to go home for the day. If this is you, self-employment may be a mistake.

One of the most challenging tasks I do daily is scheduling appointments. I didn't realize how terrible I was at this until I had to do it daily and kept screwing it up. I can look at my schedule and almost immediately forget what it says. And it's not like I have a super-complex schedule. At most, I have eight things scheduled in a day, and almost all of them start on the hour. It has taken me years to develop a system for scheduling people that cuts my mistakes down to an acceptable level. For the sake of scheduling, I have not only had to develop specific skills, but I use certain tools and also create artificial restraints in my schedule to reduce options (too many options tends to lead to mistakes). Every self-employed person I have talked to has a similar story. One person I know hates billing, which is creating and sending invoices to clients so you can get paid. Another hates asking clients to pay bills. One person hates public speaking, and another hates writing. The point is that everyone in self-employment has a task or tasks that they dislike and must do as part of their job. I love 99% of my job, but I will always have less than an absolute passion for every aspect of my job. You can mistakenly look at self-employment as freedom from the parts of your work life you don't like, but I have never seen complete liberation. I have come to terms with my limited abilities and the fact that as much as I try, I will always dislike parts of my job. If you think self-employment is all good things or will eventually be all good things for making a living, reconsider self-employment.

For the self-employed, the product (how he makes money) is himself. What does this mean? The self-employed do not have sick days or even time off. Holidays take on a new meaning. When the self-employed make money, it is because they are working. When they stop working, even for holidays, they stop making money. There are many ways to plan for this and manage this, but it is noteworthy to the average western worker that "time off" is usually paid for by the company. Also, the self-employed have no one to pick up the slack. Even if a self-employed person creates a budget that allows them to work five days a week, what if they are sick for three days? Who does that missed day of work? What if they have a family emergency that takes two weeks or two months? The US especially has laws meant to protect workers in such situations. No such laws exist for the self-employed because the product is the person. If the person gets injured or sick, there's no business. Again, one can plan for various emergencies and holidays, but the only safety net the self-employed worker has is themselves. Interestingly, I know plenty of people who left self-employment for just this reason. They were tired of trying to replace the stability of an established business with their own planning. If you don't like making such decisions or living with such uncertainties, self-employment may be a bad option.

It turns out that you are not actually all that special. I have talked with many people with good ideas who are convinced that no one has a concept like theirs. To them, it just makes sense to become self-employed because the world needs their idea, and why shouldn't they make a living off of it. The truth is that "there is nothing new under the sun." That's a quote from the Book of Ecclesiastes where the Teacher notes that life is futile and all his efforts eventually lead to nothing. Anyone who has lived long enough knows that if everyone is unique, then no one is special. Even if you have a brilliant idea, and plenty of those are out there, your "15 minutes of fame" is genuinely 15 minutes. It's temporary, and the idea is unlikely to be sufficient to create a career. So if you have a good idea or even a brilliant idea, and that is all, reconsider self-employment.

This final point may apply only to some, but even those people will not believe me until they have experienced it. Self-employment is lonely. Many of the self-employed with whom I speak report missing regular interaction with co-workers. I marveled at my friends in full-time private practice who looked forward to peer-based supervisory groups. Such groups are a best-practices–type activity where clinicians will get together weekly or monthly and discuss cases and give each other feedback on how to do effective therapy. It is an incredibly beneficial thing to do on a professional level, but what many of my friends liked about it was the social contact with other professionals. Indeed, I know many that work in clinics even though they could make far more money working independently. Many self-employed people will get lonely and consider working again for a business where they can have co-workers. Many so-called introverts posted their love stories with isolation during the first couple of months of the pandemic and then took it all back by summertime for just one night out with friends. Again, this wasn't everyone, but many people got what they thought they wanted, beautiful peace and quiet and freedom from social obligations, which turned into isolation and depression. Humans are social animals, and for that reason, self-employment might be a bad fit for you.

Checklist for self-employment

The word count for reasons you shouldn't try self-employment was more than double that of why you should. I felt this was a proper way to acknowledge the 7% self-employment rate in the US. This low number is caused by many factors and likely a combination of the work environment in the US, how workers are acculturated and trained in the US, and individual factors. With that said, self-employment makes a lot of sense for the people who are the subject of this book. Indeed, many such people are highly gifted and knowledgeable in particular areas and struggle with social interactions. I would estimate that social interactions are the most common complaint of my clients who are employed (as well as those eligible for work but not seeking employment). Self-employment just makes sense for some people.

With that said, I thought I would offer a checklist of things to measure whether or not you are ready for self-employment. Successful self-employment is almost entirely dependent on your personal preparation.

Abilities and Ideas

Do you have a unique skill set or idea? Someone once told me they wanted to start a company that would invent the time machine. The time machine is a fictitious device so far, but it is not a unique idea. This person also lacked education in physics and didn't read science fiction. Someone else told me they had an encyclopedic knowledge of Dungeons and Dragons. "So what?" I said, "What does that qualify you to do?" There is a difference between exclusive or unique and valuable. I once found a mint condition matchbox car in a box from the 70's and then gave it to my child to play with when I discovered I could get about $3 for it on eBay. I had never seen anything like it until I looked on the internet and found that even if it were relatively rare, people wouldn't pay more than $3. Your idea or skill set should be something that can generate reliable income over time. Also, when you break down how long it takes you to do something versus how much you get paid, how much per hour do you make? Someone once told me they were very excited that their friend bought a picture from them and commissioned another one. They couldn't believe that their friend would pay $20 for this thing they loved to do in their free time. It turns out that it took them four hours to make the picture. You can make twice as much with more steady work at McDonald's. That's a high price to pay for "following your passion" as a self-employed artist.

Discipline

Do you have a good record of doing things you don't want to do? For instance, how long does it take you to file your taxes? When was the last time you got an oil change on your car? When was the last time you scrubbed your shower? These are all things we can pay people money to do. We can also ignore them or just wait for other people to do them. It takes discipline to do such things yourself and on time. Can you get out of bed, even on the weekend, when you could technically sleep in? Can you shop for groceries and make dinner for yourself even when you can order delivery? How much do you deny yourself things you desire? Successful self-employment will require many decisions like this, where you choose between something you want to do and something you must do. For instance, I tell my clients I could have a huge video game system in my office. If it ever came to that, though, I would almost immediately go out of business because of my track record of getting hooked on video games. I should never have such a thing available to me during the day. Can you make such decisions? Have you? Denying myself video games was a choice I made in college so that I could pass my classes and graduate. That's part of my track record for self-discipline, and that's similar to what you need to be successfully self-employed.

Executive Functioning Skills

Self-employment is many mundane but vitally important activities. One must remember events, manage time, prioritize tasks, set goals, create plans for achieving goals, and the like. Planning and organizing are essential to making self-employment work. How did you do in high school and college, tracking your assignments and getting everything in on time and well done? This demand has always been and may always be a problem for some people. If you were able to master independently managing your work and your schedule in high school, you have a good start for self-employment. If not, get started on it.

Even if you are escaping the workplace to escape people, you will still have to work with people. Usually, those people are your customers. If you have a product or a skill set, someone has to buy it for you to make money. You might want to sell your wares online, and then you will communicate with your clients through copy, or written descriptions of your product. How you create copy matters, so there are people called copywriters who make a living from writing good copy. Whether you're self-employed or have 1000 co-workers, communication is a work essential, so you must have basic communication skills mastered.

Business Skills

I encourage you to buy a book about starting your own small business. In it, you will read about the various aspects of a small business. As I noted above, the self-employed need to know far more about business than just the product or skill they are selling. Finance is a hugely important topic, and besides psychology, it takes up the single most considerable amount of my time at work. Many people I talk to do not have a bank account. Those that do cannot access it because they do not know their password. Many of my clients tell me they don't think about money, so they don't have a bank account they can access. You need to start thinking about money. You should think about income and spending, investing, saving, and budgeting. If any of those terms are a mystery to you, get working on them right now. You likely already have some knowledge that will be useful to you in your self-employed situation like using social media, creating websites, or knowledge of computer software. Sharpen these skills but be prepared for a very steep learning curve in many other areas once you start your business.

Plan

How much money do you want to make? What will be your expenses? What will you sell, and how will you sell it? These questions are topics in any of the books you borrow from the library about how to be self-employed, and you should start answering all of them. Then, use your answers to formalize a plan for your business. You should also have a way to describe what your ultimate goal is (like a values statement or mission statement) that can guide you when decision-making gets especially complicated.

Resources

Years ago, when first becoming self-employed, I was recommended to make a list of "Gate Keepers" in my life. I'm sure this was a term from some self-help book for starting your own business. Gate Keepers are the people who have access to the people who will buy your product or expertise. In my profession, Gate Keepers are often other psychologists, doctors, and educators since most of my business comes from other professionals in my industry. Who or what are your resources beyond your knowledge or skill set? Again, when I was starting in private practice, I was able to find very cheap office space. It was so cheap it became one of my resources. Perhaps you know someone who is successfully doing the work you want to do, or you have an asset, like a car, essential to delivering your product. These are resources you should catalog. You might also discover that not having that resource is a massive barrier to self-employment. I have another friend developing a product, and a considerable obstacle is gathering the money he needs to build prototypes. An inheritance from a rich relative or a bank loan could be a resource in this case.

Work

Self-employed people tend to work more than they expect to work. Indeed, it is not uncommon for such people to do the math and discover they are making far less per hour than they had hoped. One example comes from rideshare drivers who work for companies like Uber and Lyft. The average hourly rate for such drivers is $18 in late 2021. This rate may sound like a good amount if you are a recent high school graduate since you will get less if you work at a fast-food restaurant. However, this amount does not account for gas, car repair, and other benefits like health insurance or retirement that one can get from a more standard work contract. To compensate for a low hourly rate, one must work more hours. Realtors tell me a similar story. When factoring in all the phone calls, house showings, and paperwork, the hourly rate for selling a house is relatively low. Can you currently work 40 hours a week? Even if it's "just driving people around," 40 hours a week, week after week, can be a grind. Consider that you will likely need to work more than 40 hours a week to make money in the initial months or years of self-employment.

Sustainability

Many people switch jobs every few years or even more often. This pattern is pretty standard, but considering the startup cost of being self-employed, you should consider a self-employment situation that can last longer than the average employment. Your self-employment might require an infusion of cash from a loan that will need to be paid back. You will also likely have to work more hours initially to get things up and running. Finally, you may have to buy a lot of equipment that you will have to use for a while to recoup your investment. If your initial investment of time and money is small, you will only have to run the business a short time to get a return on your investment. If startup costs are high, you need to plan for working at that business longer. For instance, my startup costs were mainly a desk and a computer. I needed to run my business for about 18 months to make up for the investment. I talked with someone who wanted to start a tree removal business. Startup costs for him would take at least five years to recoup because chain saws and cranes are expensive. Thankfully he found more than five years of tree work.

Self-employment is an excellent option for those with the skills, resources, and opportunities. However, it is not a perfect option for people simply looking to escape more traditional work environments, even if that is an added benefit. One should not enter self-employment flippantly or lightly, but with clever planning, it can be sustainable and rewarding.

Chapter 9

How Much Should Someone Work?

"I want to work as little as possible."
"I want to throw myself into my work."
"I'm worried about getting tired at work."
"I would like to have a good work/life balance."
"I want to enjoy my life and not work all the time."

These summarize some of the dozens of statements I have heard people make over the years as they work out their relationship with work. The reality is that work will not go away. It is not only necessary for living, but it is unavoidable. Those who have created imperfect substitutions for the benefit of work in their lives cannot escape the fact that society expects them to work. As a result, all people must define their relationship with work, and one of the most fundamental questions asked is how much should a person work?

What makes this question fundamental is less about its importance (even though it is essential) and more about its quantifiability. Just the other day, someone wanted to prove to me that they were a hard worker, and the single piece of evidence they used was how much they work. They worked 50-60 hours a week, but they were coming up on their busy season where they would work as many as 80 hours a week. To them, that meant they were a hard worker. By contrast, I work about 38 hours a week. If I became strapped for cash, people who know how many hours I work would immediately tell me to put in more hours. Even though the number of hours a person works is only one small piece of making sense of the importance of work in our lives, it is still a meaningful piece because it's easy to measure. So let's talk about how much to work.

Social Expectation

There are a couple of ways to define what society expects regarding the number of hours a person should work. First, I want to clarify that I am talking less about hard and fast rules and more about social norms in this section. By this, I mean that when we use a term like "full-time work," I want to describe how the average person interprets that term.

There are two basic kinds of work when categorizing work by the number of hours: part-time work and full-time work. The layperson thinks of full-time employment as at least 40 hours of work per week. This belief is based on the workweek, five days long, and the workday, eight hours long. When people talk about the workday being eight hours, they mean you are working, or "on the clock" for eight hours, and not necessarily at work for eight hours. Certain things do not count toward work, even though they happen at work.

An example of this is lunch break. There are rules around how much break time a person should receive during a work shift. Those rules can change by location, profession, and type of work. But an eight-hour workday will usually take about nine hours because a person takes about an hour of break each eight-hour shift. We traditionally talk about a "9 to 5" job, but such a job, called "shift work" is more like a "7 to 3:30" which includes 30-minutes for lunch and two 15-minute breaks.

Full-time work is often technically 38 or more hours of work every week. Some people might work at least 38 hours when they do extra work in their part-time job (e.g., if someone is sick and your boss asks you to work extra to cover for them), but this extra work does not make it a full-time job. This stipulation is critical to keep in mind since there are huge differences between working full time and part-time, even while doing the same work. In some jobs, if you work less, you will be paid less. But that magical number 38 usually differentiates jobs that include other compensation or "benefits" such as health insurance coverage or retirement plans from those that do not. Full-time jobs not only pay more money because people are working more hours, but they often include benefits that have actual, real-world value. People might think that working less than full time sounds ideal. Those people should examine what they are losing by not working full time. Extra hours at work can mean a lot of additional benefits beyond just additional pay.

Part-time work is generally not career-focused, whereas full-time work is often career-focused. Full-time work represents a commitment to a career. Part-time work usually means a commitment to something besides the work and the utility of a part-time job to bring in extra income or help occupy some time. Society expects people serious about a profession or career to work full-time. If an adult is working part-time, society usually expects them to have another job or obligation, such as raising children or going to school. Indeed, many adults who are part-time workers work far more than 40 hours per week because the part-time work adds to an already full-time obligation.

In the past couple of decades, industrialized countries like the US and many European countries have been very interested in the precise amount of time full-time workers should be working. The summary of much of the research to date is that it depends largely on cultural factors such as how societies practice the acts of work and leisure. Also, the exact number is likely pretty close to the traditional number of 40. Forty might be a little on the high end, but only by a couple of hours. Forty is close enough, from what I can tell.

Adults who work less than 40 hours are considered idle. Idleness is a negative quality. Of course, many things can cause idleness, but society sees idleness as bad. Therefore, society criticizes idle people for their idleness. On the other hand, there is a social benefit to working full time in that you escape some of the criticism of other adults. In my work with families who are transitioning children to adulthood, parents usually try to create a plan that requires their child to work 40 hours a week. This plan might include a part-time job and one or two classes in college. Parents try to account for 40 productive hours between jobs, college classes, and homework for their young adults. Less than that is only a stepping stone to achieving 40 productive hours. For those skeptical about my assessment of the value of industry (the opposite of idleness), movies and TV shows often address this topic, so be on the lookout for it. People who work less than full time get criticized for their lack of industry.

Based on cultural norms and societal expectations, I do encourage all adults to be working full time, either in a traditional 9-5 job, raising children, or some other formal pursuit. Following are some additional arguments for this recommendation.

Economic Demands

The 40-hour workweek is a cornerstone of most economies in the West. Most cultures break that 40-hour workweek into even amounts over several days. The ebb and flow of most cities are based on the understanding that adults are at work during the day. Everyone knows to go to Disneyland on a Tuesday and not on a Saturday because you'll be able to ride more rides on Tuesday. You can ride more rides because most people are at work on Tuesday but are off work on Saturday. Certain things happen during the day, such as banking, and other things happen in the evening, such as watching TV. There used to be "Primetime TV," which started at 8 pm when all the good TV shows were on. Primetime TV would never happen during the traditional 9-5 workday.

The point is that "business" generally happens during the day, especially on weekdays, and entertainment and relaxation occur in the evenings and on weekends. For the most part, this pattern follows a 40-hour workweek.

Consider the budget of the typical adult. They will pay for housing, food, transportation, clothing, entertainment, and many other expenses. Generally speaking, a person must earn a full-time wage to afford these things. Indeed, some full-time wages cannot cover all of these expenses. In that case, people are offered government financial assistance or even told to go without necessities. The point here is that not being able to afford basic life necessities even while working a full-time job is considered an exception and, in some cases, a social problem (not necessarily a problem with the individual). Indeed, if a person is financially in-need and not working a full-time job, the first piece of advice they will receive is to work more. Many politicians will make promises to adjust the economy to make commodities cheaper so that all people who work full time will be able to live comfortably. In short, they are saying that if you are achieving society's standard for work (specifically, the 40-hour workweek), they will try to make things more affordable for you. The reality is that politicians make promises to get re-elected and often have no intention of following through. The point is that when people see full-time workers struggling to make ends meet, they implicitly know that it is a problem with the economy and not necessarily the worker. Full-time work adds a layer of protection for the reputation of the average worker.

Family Expectations

If you are fortunate enough to have a family that cares about how you spend your time, you will likely discover that they want you to be productive for 40 hours a week. However, you will also find that there are many things your family wants you to do and a number they do not want you to do.

Going to college "full time" usually means taking at least 12 units, but often as much as 18-20 units (for the ambitious types). One unit usually represents one hour in class. Experts recommend spending about 2-3 hours outside of class for every hour in class, so a person taking 12 units should work at least an additional 24 hours a week on work outside of class. Twelve units equal about 36 hours of work per week, which is close to the expected 40 hours. If a person goes to school "part-time," they are typically expected to supplement their time with other productive activities. I have found that between school and these supplemental activities, like volunteerism or part-time work, the academic and other productive hours add up to about 40 hours total per week. Once a person obtains a college degree, they are typically expected to pursue a career that means full-time work. It is hard to escape the expectation of working full time.

Young adults living at home may notice several themes in their parents' desire for how the adult child spends their time. First, it is almost always the case that parents expect the child to get up at a reasonable hour, even when there is nothing scheduled that will force them to be up early. To achieve this, one must go to bed at a reasonable hour to easily wake up in the morning. Parents relax on these betimes and sleep routines on the weekend, but expect the adult child to take on increased responsibility in household chores. When a child becomes an adult, parents hope to train the adult child to living independently while accepting help on some household duties. Parents may relax while the adult child steps in to help with chores. This is seen as the child assuming an adult role in the family. Even though parents' expenses do not change, the parents should now expect the adult child to start paying for things, such as food and rent. The young adult can only achieve this with a job, and parents will often waive this expense if the adult child is in school "full time." If the adult child is in school part-time and working part-time, money for food and shelter expected from the adult child will be proportional to what they make. For instance, if the adult child only makes $400 a month, the parents may expect to be paid 30% of that ($120) for housing and perhaps 20% for food. Interestingly, this percentage is similar to how government assistance programs, such as Section 8 Housing and food stamps, determine how much to subsidize food and housing for poor individuals. Underneath it all, however, is the baseline of a 40-hour week.

"How can you stay up all night and expect to do well in school or at your job," many frustrated parents ask? Working people sleep at night and work during the day—no more up all night, no more sleeping late. As an adult, you have additional freedoms but not proportional liberties with your time. In fact, in many ways, your time gets more restricted. You might see parents questioning how many video games their adult children are playing based, not on the amount of free time they have, but on how much the adult child <u>should</u> have. Parents will look at their own lives and decide that between working 40 hours, sleeping 8 hours a night, self-care, eating, cleaning the house, and a host of other obligations, they have only about an hour or two of free time a day at best. And this is all the young adult will be allowed to play video games each day. You might say that you can find much more than a couple of hours a day for gaming, but this comes at the expense of other good and necessary things such as social life, exercise, clean house, etc. No parent ever looked at their adult child playing 6-8 hours of video games a day and said they needed to work less to maintain their gaming hobby and manage other household obligations. The 40 hours of work will always be necessary, and video games will always be the first to be cut.

Many couples, especially those without children, will choose to work full time. Even if they can establish a comfortable life with a fraction of two full-time salaries, this pattern is the case. With additional expenses and obligations, such as children, it is standard for at least one parent to work full time. The other parent will usually do at least full-time managing the household, and if that takes less than full time, they will get another part-time obligation. No one thinks it is ok for a spouse to have less than a full-time obligation in their lives. Many parents whose primary responsibility is to raise children will talk about attempts to manage their time when children grow and start attending school or otherwise become more independent. Many such parents choose this time to go back to working a full-time job if they initially stopped such work to manage the household. Even with the combined work potential of a married couple, both of those people still expect, in most situations, to be working 40 hours a week at something- either full-time work at an office or full-time household management, or some combination of that. Interestingly, 40 hours of productive work per week often continues well after children have left the house (i.e., empty nest) and other major expenses are taken care of (e.g., house mortgage paid off).

Kids expect at least one of their parents to be at a job during the day. So when this parent comes home unexpectedly during the day, it's a big deal. This expectation happens both before and after the child can understand that adults work 40 hours per week. I have listened to many people reflect on their childhood and talk about their parents' work patterns. The standard they use to decide if it's too much or not enough work is the 40-hour work week. If the parent worked less, they feel compelled to explain why their parents are not lazy. If the parent worked more, they explain why the parent is not neglectful. People use the 40-hour-per-week expectation to determine what excuse to make.

Quality of life

How does one promote quality of life with this notion of 40 hours per week of work in view? There are two questions to ask to make this estimation.

What other things besides work do you want to do?

Nothing, and anything. These are the two extreme responses. Some people want their whole life to be about work. These people will sometimes sleep at work or work when they're home. Any relationship they have will support their work, and any interests they have will be limited by their jobs. On the other extreme (e.g., I would prefer to do anything but work), people will try to do as little as possible to meet their financial needs. They will look for jobs that require very little actual work or very little energy to perform. These people tend to despise any kind of work because it gets in the way of what they really want to be doing. For the person who wants nothing but to work, the more they work, the higher their quality of life. For those who want to do anything but work, the less they work, the higher their quality of life. Both extremes, however, are tough to achieve, so I do not recommend either of them. Instead, I recommend you enjoy your work and have enjoyable activities that are not part of your job. The ratio of those things you enjoy that are work and not work will often dictate how much you work relative to the 40-hour work week.

What are the limiting factors of your situation?

The intensity of your work will also dictate how much and when you work. For instance, firefighters tend to work several days in a row. Indeed, they sometimes have to sleep at work, but the times they are awake are incredibly intense, so their time actively pulling people out of burning buildings is not likely 40 hours per week on average. In private practice, I only spend about half to ¾ of my time "at work" in a session with a client. The other times I'm usually completing paperwork or writing this book. Many office jobs offer a modest but steady flow of work all day. Based on your temperament, preferences, experience, and the flow of work, you might find 40 hours of work too easy or extremely challenging, which will affect your quality of life.

Compensation can make a big difference to the quality of life. As I said earlier, some people work full time but do not make enough to support even a modest lifestyle. Low pay can keep a person from saving money, paying for healthcare, buying a house or car, paying off debt, or other essential things for healthy living in this country. Such people might not want to work more, but they have to work more to afford such things. Others might need to work more but are limited in some way, such as transportation, opportunity, or health. As much as we would like to choose to work more or less, our situation often dictates how much we must work or how little we can work. Sometimes we have a low quality of life because of work and despite our desires.

The myth of retirement

The final statement I want to make is cautionary about the end of the work-life, otherwise known as retirement. The current average retirement age (for those born after 1960) in the US is 67 years old. 67 is when many financial and governmental rules kick in, and people can traditionally retire or stop working full time. This age is important because financial advisors will use age 67 to help you plan for your retirement. By the age of 67, they will tell you that you need to have saved a certain amount of money to enjoy your life and stop working all the time.

There are many things to consider when thinking about retirement. First, your expenses make a massive difference in your quality of life when you retire. If you own your house vs. live in an apartment at age 67, this has a significant impact on your standard of living. Indeed there are a bunch of such expenses that one can have or not have when they retire. These expenses are not things like vacations or TV subscriptions, so-called discretionary spending. They are non-discretionary expenses such as housing, healthcare, and debt. When thinking about how much you should work or which jobs you should work to meet your budget, consider that there are budget items now that will be critical decades down the road. If you ever want to stop working, you must plan for that time right now. Consult a financial adviser to get started on this ASAP. Also, even if you achieve financial stability by age 67, you might not be healthy enough to enjoy it or have anyone to enjoy it with. Consider those factors when you're thinking about how to spend your time now.

The second consideration is that you might not want to stop working at 67. In college, I learned about the "terminal drop." A large subset of people dies within five years of retirement. This idea of a carefree, exciting, and entertaining retirement jet-setting around the world and sitting on beaches seems to be the reality for very few people. It is undoubtedly not the phenomenon popular media seems to tell us it is. And this makes sense, too, since this type of retirement requires a whole industry, including financial planners, banks, vacation resorts, and airlines. Advertising sensationalizes "the good life" at age 67, so beware of the fantasy elements of retirement. It is not uncommon for people to live 15 to 20 or more years after retiring. In some cases, this is a whole separate career in itself. One can only vacation so long before it's no longer a vacation.

In conclusion

If you choose to work more or less than 40 hours per week as an adult, you will likely fight the norm. For many people I talk to, this makes little difference since they have been fighting standards all their lives. But I hope I made a case for swimming with the stream this time. Applying to the 40-hour-per-week norm will make many other things in your life easier—from maintaining your reputation with others to getting enjoyment and fulfillment out of your life, to achieving current and future financial goals. There is much to be gained from being with the group on the issue of how much to work. So, I hope you will consider this issue diligently and act according to your values and goals.

Chapter 10

Balancing Work and Life

What does work/life balance mean?

Work/life balance is a term that refers to a concept and not a specific thing. It is a term that most people use and implicitly know what it means. Most people who hear this term understand what it refers to, so you also need to know how to use it correctly. You will need this term to understand what people are talking about, but more importantly, to apply it to your own life.

This morning, the News reported that Gavin Newsom, the current governor of California, took a short break from public life because his young children held an "intervention" for him over dinner one night. It was reported that they were concerned that he would miss Halloween because of work, and they were not having it. Newsom has had a terrible year (or a couple of years). He governs the largest state in the Union and, in his term, has dealt with the pandemic, social unrest, and unprecedented wildfires and drought, among other things. Newsome said his state has gone "from crisis to crisis" over the past couple of years, and he felt he was on a treadmill with his job. Recently, he battled a "recall vote," which was defeated, meaning he gets to keep doing his job. In short, his job is challenging in good times (it has not been good times) and he just fought for the ability to continue working for many people that do not like him. Newsom's children told their dad he had a problem with work/life balance. He needed some help with his priorities because he was planning to do the inconceivable: skip Halloween.

So what do people mean when they talk about maintaining a proper work/life balance? Isn't work part of life? I admit that the concept can get very complicated if you think about it. Even though people probably refer to a host of factors, their decision about work/life balance probably comes down to a feeling. Work/life balance being primarily a feeling makes the concept so hard for some people to understand. Newsom stated that he woke up with "that knot in [my] stomach"[3] one morning and knew something was off with this balance. For Newsom, the knot in his stomach was not from bad takeout the night before, an ulcer, or worries about any future event. That knot was likely the conflict between work and life, or what he wanted to do and what he needed to do. Here are some factors people consider when determining if they have a proper work/life balance.

Time

In the simplest terms and using perhaps the most straightforward metric, people consider how much time they spend working vs. doing other things. Again, the general standard is a third of your time working, a third sleeping, and a third everything else. This metric excludes weekends, of course, but on weekends people usually do other productive things like weekly tasks (shopping, mowing the lawn) and family/social things (going to church, taking kids to the park). It is easy, especially in one's career, to let the third of your time devoted to working increase and eclipse other parts of your life. For instance, many people commute to work. Some people commute great distances for work but do not count it as part of the work day. They often take the commute time out of sleeping or "everything else" time. Anyone who has been on public transportation early in the morning will see people sleeping. Other people will be playing games. These are examples of how we compensate for the loss of time that can be the morning or evening commute-we'll try to do other things during

---

[3] https://www.msn.com/en-us/news/us/gavin-newsom-says-he-canceled-trip-to-climate-summit-after-intervention-from-his-kids/ar-AAQw6Ya Accessed July 30, 2022.

this time. Long commutes or extended working hours such as earlier mornings, later evenings, or working on weekends can seriously disrupt the work/life balance. Interestingly, this disruption is always in the direction of working too much, never "lifing" too much.

Finances

Many people have the option to make more money if they work more. I have said elsewhere that promotions at work often come with a pay increase. This promotion almost always comes with increased responsibility, often expressing itself in additional work time. More pay can be great, but more time working is not always great. A person might take the increased income and justify the increased amount of work because they have something they want to buy. Unfortunately, most people use more money to buy things they don't need. The classic example of this is the newly promoted worker that can now afford to buy the boat he always wanted but can never sail that boat because he's always at work. People can refer to this as a "financial treadmill" where they can never seem to "get ahead" on their finances. Often it is because people tend to increase their spending for discretionary expenses when they have an increase in income. They think they are improving their quality of life with these discretionary expenses. All things being equal, they may be doing just that if they had the increased time to enjoy their boats.

Phase of life

Most people make decisions about how much they work while making decisions about other seminal events in their lives.

Marriage

People generally start their careers around the same time they get married or start long-term romantic relationships. However, forming, establishing, and maintaining a marriage or other long-term relationships takes considerable time and resources. Therefore, most people do not choose between working on their career or working on their marriage-they must balance their efforts for both simultaneously.

Children

Have you ever heard about a job that requires three to five years of experience? Do you know what happens about three to five years after getting married? Most people have children by this time. Common sense and research say the physical presence of parents matters in a child's life. Parents just "bringing home the bacon" and then watching the TV in the evening are not being adequate parents; we just pretend they are. Add to that the fact that children are aging and growing, and the opportunity to be physically present when they are four years old lasts only one year. Perhaps that's when you are offered a promotion or, God forbid, get fired and need to look for a new job and start working that job. You cannot at the same time work more and be physically and emotionally present for your child. How much of that "everything else" time that you can spend with your child do you want to spend at work?

Health

When people hit the fives and tens, like 35 and 40 years old, they almost always note that their body requires more maintenance than it used to. For instance, people who could get by on five or six hours of sleep a couple of nights a week now report they cannot get less than eight hours of sleep and be productive at work. "Burning the candle at both ends" goes from risky to deadly for some people. Borrowing from sleep or "everything else" time to work becomes more and more costly the older a person gets. Such borrowing may no longer be an option, and the work/life balance that could always favor work is no longer sustainable.

Expenses

Even though people may be motivated to work less as they age, many people find their expenses increasing due to many social or health factors. Healthcare and aging children living at home almost always mean increased costs. Have you ever heard of a midlife crisis? Many people will report the tension between increasing responsibilities and decreasing resources during their 40s and 50s. Sometimes this tension causes an existential crisis, but this usually causes increased stress which individuals must address. Often a work/life imbalance will be blamed for the stress, but the challenge is that there is no easy solution in this situation. For example, if I work less, I make less. If I make less, I default on my financial responsibility. But I can't work more because I have less to give. Do you see the tension?

Hobbies

Everyone believes they should be able to enjoy their lives. It is odd for a person to have no interests other than work. Even if a person's interests are related to their work, people will report the importance of doing an activity because they choose to do it and not because they are paid or otherwise obliged. This concept is what the phrase "you owe it to yourself" means. Being independent, in control, autonomous, or willful is a massive issue for everyone who is, ever was, or ever will be. To maintain work/life balance, we must regularly have the feeling of doing things in a seemingly unfettered state. To feel balanced, we must be able to do something because we choose to do it and not because we are obliged to do it. This choice often comes in the form of hobbies. Objectively speaking, hobbies are often inconsequential, but no one thinks they are unnecessary. Hobbies are almost exclusively the domain of that "everything else" category of time. Hobbies almost always get axed when time gets tight, but I think this is an existentially dangerous precedent. Autonomy is part of the identity of all humans, and removing activities that satisfy our need for autonomy will, over time, create problems in other areas of our lives. One can borrow time from hobbies, but one should never eliminate hobby time for too long.

Vacations and Holidays

Two weeks of paid vacation is standard in American society, but the average amount of paid vacation for the average American is lower than that. It was probably not long ago that employers added vacation time to a worker's compensation as a benefit, like health insurance. We know from experience and research that failure to take breaks in the form of holidays and vacations can dramatically reduce a person's productivity, even to the point of incapacitation and death. People who work-work-work tend to die earlier than those that do not. This pattern is true for people who never take vacations. It is also true for people who stare at a computer for eight hours straight and never stand up and walk around the office. During the recent pandemic, travel was restricted, and many simply chose to keep working. Initially, there was a bump in productivity as people skipped vacations and eliminated their commutes. However, the tail end of those decisions seems to be creating fatigue, burnout, and loss of productivity or even exiting the workforce. It's good to take breaks not just because you dislike your job and need something to get you through the day, but because it helps you work harder and longer when you're not on vacation. Even though vacation is a relatively new concept for the everyday worker, we have celebrated in the form of holidays (and time off from labor) for millennia since the beginning of time. It's tough to fight taking a holiday–it's in our blood.

Rest

On a separate but related note, try as we might, we cannot help but sleep. The same goes for physical rest. Our bodies and our brains need time off from work to recuperate. Pro-football players have noted that adding a Thursday night football game (games only took place on Sundays and Mondays until recently) significantly increases the chance of injuries. Professionals are predicting that this additional game night will also shorten the careers of many good players who have to be ready to perform on this additional day. The apparent world record for staying awake was 11 days, set in 1965 by a 17-year-old for a science fair. Lack of sleep causes significant cognitive declines that tend to resolve, for the most part, after a couple of nights of sleep. Chronic lack of sleep, however, seems to be related to permanent cognitive declines in the form of dementia or other brain disorders. The point is that people can borrow from sleep or other restful activities that happen in the "everything else" category, but extensive borrowing is impossible and sometimes has catastrophic consequences. Feeling tired all the time, having chronic body pain or low energy, or having trouble focusing or concentrating can all be caused by improper work/life balance.

Loving your work

As critical as people seem about work, most people I know either like or love working. However, I have certainly talked with people who either like or are ambivalent about working but seriously hate their jobs. One of the high costs of upsetting the balance between work and other things is coming to despise your job. This outcome is, in a sense, a paradox because it is the working of the job that causes the person to hate the job. Working the right amount results in liking or loving the job, but too much work may breed hate. Interestingly, some people love their job and want to work it more. These are the truly fortunate people for whom going to work is enjoyable. They protect this love for work by placing more emphasis on the life portion of the balance.

Health

It is worth repeating that it is not uncommon for a person's work and health to be at odds. Health concerns may cause some workers to feel less than their best at work. For other workers, if their health issues become even more severe their work life may be devastated. A person can develop a health condition due to failure to balance work and life. For instance, heart disease can result from increased stress and lack of exercise. Other people have pre-existing or chronic health and mental health conditions that preclude them from certain rigors of work. As much as such people would like to work more than they do, or even really need to work more, their health keeps them from that. In this case, much like other meaningful relationships, a person adds more to one area at the expense of the other. For instance, certain health conditions mean that working more increases poor health. Or, focusing on improving one's health means less attention to work. As a result, workers cannot successfully negotiate some of these trades, making sacrifice inevitable.

Conclusion

How then shall we work and live? I have discovered that the average worker occasionally has a feeling that the work/life balance needs adjustment and usually in the direction of less work. Many of the people I work with find it helpful to examine and understand the relevant variables in order to move forward with creating a plan to balance work and life. Be careful about looking at these listed variables as exhaustive, though. How I developed them was to look at my own life and take note of those things that have had push/pull relationships in my life. I encourage the reader to think about things you must experience outside of work, something you value, or things you desire, and add those to the "life" section of work/life balance. For example, how satisfied are you with how you spend your time? Perhaps you have much time for hobbies but have no plans for long-term financial stability. Maybe it's the other way around: you feel compelled to be financially stable as soon as possible, and you are sacrificing the enjoyment and balance that will increase your quality of life and promote your productivity.

The other thing to note goes back to the conceptual rather than literal nature of the work/life balance. Even though you likely understand what your peers are talking about when discussing work/life balance, you are probably not talking about the same set of variables that you will ultimately change to enhance that balance. This difference is acceptable because, more than advice, people want to know that others understand their challenges. You may not be able to get advice, but you can get (and give) encouragement, which is usually far more helpful than clever advice. The point is that too often we reject the advice, ideas, or counsel of our friends because their experiences feel too far removed from our own. In such cases, your "list" might look different, but your desire for balance is the same. Listen to the experience and ideas of others and gain what knowledge and understanding you can.

Finally, achievement of work/life balance is a moving target. This fact is essential to know for a couple of reasons. First, you will likely never be completely satisfied with the balance you have achieved. You will have days you are tired or bored, days you are frustrated, or days when your desires suddenly shift. One should look for general satisfaction or set a "good enough" standard for this balance. Indeed, some people can spend too much time trying to achieve a perfect balance, and the extended effort at balancing can throw off the balance. The second issue to consider is that your matrix of needs, resources, values, and desires will change over time. Some people realize, seemingly all of a sudden, that their work/life balance is off and decide they are having a crisis. In reality, we can predict that this balance will need regular tending, and we should not be surprised when there is a noticeable and stable change in our assessment of this balance. I cannot give any hard and fast rules for when to manage this balance, but some people set aside regular times for reflection on this issue (e.g., birthdays or anniversaries; New Year's Day; vacations). I consider this issue every time I have a significant failure at work or home. Perhaps this failure has resulted because my work/life balance needs adjustment. Self-examination from both an emotional and rational perspective, and not just one or the other, is a good practice, and I can commend it to you.

Chapter 11

Career Advancement

It is possible but unlikely that your first job will be your last job. You will likely have various jobs over your career, even if you stay within the same field. People indeed get new jobs because they lose (e.g., get fired or laid off) their old ones, but many people pursue or get offered new jobs that are supposed to be better, in some way, than their previous job. In many cases, such moves from job to job can be considered career advancement.

What is career advancement?

How does one's career advance or otherwise move forward? Advancement is a strange concept to contemplate and another example of an idea that people understand but might struggle to describe. As abstract as it might be, career advancement is often one of the main driving forces in people's work lives. People often work for the sake of advancing their careers. If a person defines their career as "a job or profession that someone does for a long time," then the advancement of that thing makes it better in some way. Whether or not a career is better is a subjective assessment, so it might be better to list some of the objective identifiers people use to decide whether or not they are advancing in their career. Please note that not all of these are positive (i.e., more of something). Some are undoubtedly negative (i.e., less of something).

Increased pay

Getting paid more to do the same job or work within the same career indicates career advancement. Hourly workers can indeed make more money by working more hours. In this case, more pay is not career advancement, but more hours may be.

More hours

I tell my clients that being scheduled for fewer hours or fewer shifts in hourly employment is typically a bad sign. But, on the other hand, more opportunities to work can often mean that you have more trust or preference with your supervisor. They want you to work more because you do good work.

Increased specialization

In many professions, increased specialization is a sign of career advancement. The fewer people who can do your job the better. Exclusivity is often a good thing professionally, and people can cause a specialization in their work by increasing their training and certification, which will, in many cases, advance their career.

Less "grunt work"

In every profession, there is work people prefer not to do. Tedious, gross, or dangerous tasks are those people generally prefer to do less or not at all. So having someone who gets you your coffee instead of getting it yourself can signify career advancement. Newer employees typically get "grunt work".

Consultation

Consultation is a peculiar category of work. This is consultation: you get paid to tell people how they should do their job but are not responsible if they don't do it (like a supervisor might be). People can get so good at their jobs that people will pay them to learn how they got so good. They pay you for your opinions. Increased solicitation for your opinion could be a sign of advancement. Let me be clear that unsolicited opinions (i.e., giving an opinion when no one is asking) could work against a person. Only solicited opinions count in this case.

Perks

When people advance in their careers, sometimes companies encourage workers to stay with the company and not look at other jobs. Businesses can do this in many ways, but one way is through perks or unique advantages to working for this company and not another. For instance, a friend was offered a "company car" if he would accept a supervisory position. In addition, some companies give their workers "expense accounts" to buy food on work trips. Perks come in many forms, but something you get that other workers don't get is a perk and could be a sign of advancement.

Investment

Sometimes companies will pay for things that make you better at your job. For instance, they might pay for specialized training or an expensive machine that will allow you to further specialize (see above) in your work. People spending money to help you improve your work performance can signify advancement.

Notoriety

All industries have their so-called famous people. I could list a handful of famous psychologists that no one other than psychologists has ever heard of (and it's not Dr. Phil). I am sure there are renowned air traffic controllers, plumbers, and endocrinologists. Being more well-known in your field is a sign of career advancement. Side-note on this issue: it's best if you're well known in your field for being good at your job and not necessarily something unrelated.

More good, less bad

This category can be tough to measure. Sometimes people will draw back on some aspect of their work to get more of the type of work they want. For instance, I worked on one landscaping crew where the more senior workers got to use the riding lawnmowers, and the junior crew members had to use the push mowers. In general, however, doing more of the work you like and less of what you don't, or even having more choice about spending your time working, can be a good sign of career advancement.

Driving forces of advancement

What makes careers advance? More specifically, if I wanted to advance in my career, how would I do it?

Again, this is an area where there is more than one answer, and the list I will provide is not exhaustive. However, any of these items by themselves is great, and all of them working together are best.

Time (Achieving Seniority)

Time may be the most decisive influence on career advancement. Namely, the longer you do something, the more you advance at it. Time can be both a guarantee and a requirement for promotion. The longer a person works, in any job, the more seniority they have. Companies often use seniority to decide how much new people should get paid. A new hire with a lot of experience will usually get paid more than a new hire with little experience doing the same job. So, if you want to advance in your career, do your job for as long as possible without getting fired or demoted. Unsolicited demotions are an obvious setback in career advancement. In many cases, being fired is more like a reset in career advancement—people who get fired either regress to a lower place in their career or switch careers altogether.

Doing even a mediocre job for a long time almost always leads to career advancement. Advancement happens in this case because people passively acquire "experience" over time that is valuable to the company. People usually only have to be taught to do a specific job once, and even if they need reteaching, the relearning is much faster than the initial learning. This process all adds up to profitability for the company, which eventually works in the worker's favor in the mode of career advancement. Also, the longer you are around, the more opportunity you have to be offered specific jobs or positions within the company as they become available. Time is this great engine that has an indelible effect on everything, including your career. Rather than wearing it out, however, time seems to mature or advance one's career.

Good Work (Building a Positive Reputation)

When I was a landscaper at a certain unnamed university where I would work summers, I was a member of the part-time work crew. This crew mainly was other college students home from college and somehow related to someone that worked at the university. Expectations for work were not high, and it was pretty hard to get fired. In the morning, the part-time crew would take the first hour after punching in to pick up trash around campus. This assignment was absurd during the summer because the campus was mostly a ghost town since very few people lived in the dorms. No one generated much trash to pick up. The roughly 15 of us would clock in at 7 am, grab our trash bag from the roll, and head out of the shop. About 14 of those workers would head to many different student lounges and hang out and talk for an hour. They would then stroll back to the shop and toss empty trash bags in the dumpster. It was a morning ritual. On the other hand, I would walk a circuit around the campus that took me about an hour. I would occasionally find a piece of trash or two, but mostly it was a pleasant morning stroll for me.

As I said, no one got fired, and everyone knew there was little trash to pick up. The full-time guys knew where to find the 14 part-time workers if anything needed their attention. Not surprisingly, I was eventually promoted to Part-time Captain. This example might seem simplistic, but I want to point out that I didn't do anything other than my job to get promoted over 14 other equally qualified workers. But, by doing my job, I was achieving way more than those who set out to do as little of their job as possible. Even though there was very little trash to collect, walking around and looking for it and simply looking like I was working was a good job. I am amazed, all these years and all these jobs later, how reluctant many people are to do what they agreed to do when hired for a job. Like time, doing a good job is a simplistic factor in career advancement.

Notice I did not write "great work" in the title above. It is advisable to do great work when you can, but doing good work at all times is the goal. For those of you who have not worked a long time, you might not be able to fully appreciate the value of a co-worker who reliably does their job. Others of you might wonder why I'm making such a big deal out of doing good work. You might think that the goal is to get paid as much as you can for doing as little as you can. This is the goal, by the way, of the worst kind of worker. No one wants to work with such a person, and supervisors dread supervising them because they are unreliable and require a lot of management. Setting the standard for yourself to do good work at all times will advance your career by making you a desirable co-worker and employee. Supervisors will want other workers to work like you, so you may be put in charge and offered other perks to keep up the good work.

Communication (Talk and Write Good[4])

Communication in this sense is different than self-promotion. Self-promotion is simply: promoting the self. This section discusses career advancement, which focuses on what's suitable for the people to whom you're promoting yourself. Other people, either the customer or the supervisor, advance one's career. For instance, being clear about your skills and experience will help the right companies want to hire you for the correct positions. Likewise, effective advertising will bring the right clients. For example, I talked with someone that wanted to work at a store he hated but had the best pay. I told the person immediately that they wouldn't be hired because they could not hide the fact that they disliked the store. It would have been better for this

---

[4] This is a play on words.

person to be honest about his goals and get hired at a place he liked, even for less pay.

Elsewhere in this book, I talked about a friend that would do an annual job search despite loving his current employment. This activity forced him to update his resume and think about his goals. He also did interviews that allowed him to practice responses to questions about experience and goals. The good that came out of this process was developing his communication which led directly to career advancement. If someone offered him a better job, even if he liked his current position, he could take it and advance his career. Unlike "time" above, the communication factor is more active and under the worker's control. Therefore, a worker can work on communication skills.

Communication skills can also advance one's career indirectly. Communicating effectively with your work peers, people below you, and people above you in the hierarchy can improve your reputation and give you "preference" with other workers. By this, I mean that when people are looking around the office to see who they want to work with, the people they choose have a higher preference. You want to be one of those more highly preferred people for career advancement. In my work, calling people back right after they message me increases my preference among clients and peers in my field. There is a considerable difference between the psychologist people can reach by phone and those they cannot. I don't just get more clients; I have a better reputation among professionals in the field in general, which results in more referrals. I also use this standard to choose contractors to fix my roof and accountants to manage my taxes. It's the effective communicators that not only get my business but also get my preference (i.e., positive reviews). Communication skills are a powerful determinant for career advancement.

Rather than a behavior, I use the term openness to describe a state of mind or way of approaching a problem. Openness does not mean simply taking every offered job or promotion. Taking every job offer does not necessarily result in career advancement. On the other hand, responding to an opportunity (e.g., a job offer) with a sense of possibility is a way one can advance in their career. If you surveyed 10 successful career people on how they ended up in their jobs, nine out of 10 would likely say they never planned to be in their current position. They will probably tell you they have their current job because they kept an open mind and were slow to dismiss ideas that didn't meet their preconceptions. This course is true for me because I never set out to be in private practice. Psychotherapy was one of the last things I wanted to do since I assumed I would not enjoy it, or not be good at it (I had seen too many movies about therapists). However, two jobs I was offered and ended up taking pointed me in my current direction. Neither of these jobs was one I thought I could or would even want to do. Part of the decision to take the job was desperation (I had few other choices), and the other part was my investigation about the jobs. Once it looked like I met the basic requirements for the job, I researched to see if it was worth applying. Once offered the job, I researched more to know if I should take it. The process of landing both jobs required flexibility for me which was uncharacteristic (according to people who know me). Still, this openness to experiencing something outside my expectations put me on the path I am now. Openness to experience is a great personality trait to have and one that you can use all the time, but in my case, I used it very effectively twice in critical moments. Otherwise, flexibility is not one of my strongest characteristics.

Openness and flexibility in career advancement are crucial because many readers might have been described as rigid and inflexible. I know this because I work with many autistic people, and I have also been described as rigid and inflexible (even though I don't think I'm autistic). I think a person can work on being more flexible if they think it is worth the effort. Regarding career advancement, I think it's worth the effort.

What happens as people advance in their careers?

In the 1980s, psychologist Raymond Cattell developed a theory of intelligence where he described two types of intelligence: Fluid Intelligence and Crystallized Intelligence. An act of Fluid Intelligence is problem-solving based on logic and innovation, and an act of Crystallized Intelligence is problem-solving based on experience. Cattell and others report that all people operate with a mixture of both types of intelligence in all situations. Still, the dominance of one type over the other can be predicted using a person's age. Specifically, younger people use more Fluid Intelligence, and older people use more Crystallized Intelligence. This theory helps make sense of the age disparity in industries such as tech and academics. Tech is known for innovation and is also known for a youthful workforce. On the other hand, academics is known as a knowledge center, and the stereotype of the college professor is a white-haired individual with glasses and a cardigan who operates out of experience.

Of course, there are older people working in tech and younger people teaching in colleges. As you progress in your career, however, you will likely notice that the nature of your work and how you do that work will change. Specifically, as a younger worker, you will be hired for your energy, and as an older worker, you will be employed (or retained) for your experience. I bring this up here because I want you to have a framework for understanding how your career might change over time.

Young Workers

Young adults almost always comment on the same thing when they embark on their first major job search. They tell me about the "needs experience" paradox of the requirements for application to any job. All the jobs they want require 3-5 years' experience, but there are no jobs out there that will hire people with no experience so they can get the experience to get hired for the job they want. I usually advise my clients to be good communicators in these cases. For instance, I tell them to reflect on their lives and see if they have any experience, even in chores parents assigned them to do growing up, that they could talk about in an interview. The point is that employers will often look at the estimated age of an interviewee and automatically adjust expectations for experience level. It is true that some jobs rigidly or necessarily require experience, so very young interviewees with limited experience will likely not get hired. Still, many interviewers keep that in mind that young interviewees may lack experience, but possess other valuable assets. Companies value young employees for their teachability and their energy. It is also true that young employees can be good at thinking outside the box in jobs requiring creativity and innovation. The most physically rigorous work you will do will likely be in the job you have in your 20s and 30s. These are jobs with intensive, expansive training and other low-level "grunt" work expectations. Grunt work, for the record, is named because of the noise you make while doing the work. I worked for one summer as a young adult for a mason (i.e., bricklayer). It was one of the physically most demanding jobs I have ever had because I was the guy who carried all bricks and mortar from the big pile at the corner of the job site to where the masons were building a wall. I constructed the scaffolding and then carried each brick up the scaffolding to where the bricklayers were adding bricks to the wall. By lunch on my first day, I was exhausted and in significant pain, and I still had 5-6 more hours of work before quitting time. It was interesting that there were other "grunt" workers like myself there but with more seniority who were happy to see me because they no longer had to carry bricks up the scaffolding.

Young professionals should also expect to work longer hours and do the jobs other senior professionals no longer want to do. In addition, many industries depend on the energy and need for experience of young professionals.

Mid-career Workers

Mid-career workers are the majority of the workforce as they represent the middle of the energy/experience continuum. I have no specific ages when a person moves into and out of this category. Mid-career workers have to start dealing with the limitations placed on them by other essential aspects of life. Mid-career workers are those that get married and start families. They buy houses and cars. Mid-career workers can discover their education or experience is lacking and make decisions to rectify that by returning to school or switching jobs. Mid-career workers have aging bodies and brains that require more maintenance and care.

Mid-career workers notice they cannot work as much as they used to or cannot be as focused on careers at the expense of other things in their lives as they were as young workers. The fact is that Mid-career workers must confront the limitations of their physical bodies as well as the other decisions they have made. For instance, many parents would like to spend time with their children rather than work through dinner each night. Mid-career workers discover that all-nighters are no longer physically possible for them. Mid-career workers find that their bodies have aged, and this makes a difference in the amount of energy they have.

Mid-career workers, by necessity, have to shift from being a worker dependent on energy to one with increasing dependence on experience. Some people I talk to have mottos like "Work smart, not hard" or "Efficiency over energy." The reality is that even if people in this category wanted to work more or harder, they simply could not. So they either shift to being a "smart" worker that relies more and more on experience or get used up and eventually burn out. I can think of numerous examples, both personally and professionally, where a worker in this stage hit a physical limit and had to rethink how to make it through the next couple of decades of work intact.

Older Worker

Leadership favors experience. This trend is why so many CEOs are older people. Indeed, it is the exception for a young person to get hired as a CEO or a pro-football coach. For many people, making the shift successfully from primarily energy-based working to experience-based working is necessary. Companies care little about employees' health, and many older workers tell me that their job will consume them unless they put limits on their work.

As an older worker, you might notice that younger workers spend considerable time solving problems that you were able to avoid altogether. You might see that your work style is far more efficient than that of a younger worker. You might also notice that you would never agree to do an assignment that younger workers seem eager to do. To you, it looks dull, monotonous, or laborious (i.e., the definition of grunt work). Still, to the younger worker, perhaps it seems like an opportunity to gain experience or advance their career. Older workers simply work differently than younger workers. In many cases, they seem to work faster because there is less new information with each situation they deal with-less ramp-up and new learning involved. For the most part, younger workers are sprier, but not necessarily faster in their work. However, the work world values the older worker's experience.

The work world expects an increase in experience and a decrease in overall energy output as you age, even if the productivity expectations remain the same. The point is that there is a place for everyone in the work world based on their experience (or inexperience). That expectation does change over time, but the work world values energy and enthusiasm just like they value knowledge and experience. Both ends of the energy/experience continuum are vital, and all workers will predictably shift, over time, in their balance of the two extremes.

Chapter 12

Financial Planning

The point of this chapter is to encourage people who tend to be non-materialistic to become a little more materialistic. I don't think it's the case that my clients, being non-materialistic, are necessarily more moral than materialistic people. I think it has to do mainly with the phrase, "there's nothing I want to buy." This is the response I get when I ask ASD teens why they don't have a part-time job. The reality is that there are things we must buy. However, buying something you must buy does not make you materialistic. Materialism is generally about buying stuff you do not need. In the case of the ASD individuals I work with, not buying things you need seems more related to executive functioning problems. So, this chapter is for the executive functioning challenged non-materialist. Let's start with three vignettes that will describe the issue.

Vignette 1

Parents of a grade-school child with ASD express a common frustration when putting together a behavior plan in my office. "There's nothing he wants," they tell me in response to my survey on "rewards." Effective rewards are essential to a behavior modification plan. All people need motivation, even if it's motivation to do something good. It's in the rewards section of the plan that intervention with ASD children tends to fall apart. Parents of neurotypical children report that money is an adequate reward in children as young as kindergarten. Parents of ASD children, even in their teens, note that there's "nothing he wants to buy." The ASD teen will confirm this fact in questioning. I once asked a 20-year-old with

ASD how much money it would take to get him on an airplane to go somewhere fun. He was nervous about airplanes and about changing his routine. We eventually settled on $500 to get on the plane. He said he figured with $500 he could probably find something he wanted to buy. If it takes $500 to get him on a plane to someplace fun, how much would it take to get him to go to work?

Vignette 2

Research states that a part-time job is one of the best ways to prepare high schoolers and young adults for work-life in adulthood. Despite this, most high schoolers I talk to turn down the support for finding a part-time job because all they get from it is experience and money. I take them through the "thought experiment" of being able to buy whatever video game they wanted, paying for insurance and gas to drive the family car, or going to movies or comic book conventions. None of this ever works as an incentive since there's nothing they want to buy, or at least nothing worth doing the work to get the money to buy that thing. Most tell me they saved several thousand dollars from birthdays and holiday gifts. One person told me she had a big wad of cash in an envelope in a shoe box until a parent found it and forced her to open a bank account. She said, "I honestly forgot it was there."

Vignette 3

I have worked with many young professionals early in their careers who live at home. I have three general questions I ask them. How much do you get paid? How much money do you have? And finally, what are your plans for your money? The answer to these questions is the same: I don't know. Most of them do not know how to check their account balance when I prompt them because they don't know the password. One of them discovered as a 25-year-old that he couldn't call the bank to inquire about his balance because it was a "child account" and he needed a parent to grant access.

This chapter is not about financial planning. Instead, it is about the need for financial planning. There are a couple of realities why you must engage in financial planning. The first is that you will receive money in exchange for working. In fact, as the birthday envelope example above suggests, you may also receive money for surviving another year. Second, most people do not want to work until they die. Working when you're very old is tiring and gets very challenging. You think working hard now is a drag. Try working like this at age 90. Third, you may want to do things in the future that will require financial planning right now, like getting married, buying a house, having kids, and retiring. Financially "living in the moment" is an excellent way to achieve nothing that requires money because that is not how finances work.

How is this an executive functioning problem?

The second word in "financial planning" is the key to understanding this challenge. Planning is an executive functioning activity. In the case of retirement, one has to examine many variables at the moment and then think about many variables in the far future. For instance, you must consider how much money you make now and your expenses. This consideration will help you determine whether or not you need to adjust your current budget to make more money available to save. Then, you need to think about what your budget might look like in 40 years. If you do not know your current budget (how much you spend each month, and on what), considering what it *might* be in 40 years should seem impossible. Next, you must figure out how you must manage your current budget to save enough to match your future budget. Finally, there are more than a couple of ways to save money. Putting it in an envelope on your shelf might be one of the worst ways to save. Letting it passively accrue interest in a bank savings account might not give you enough return to match your budget in 40 years. The point is that it gets very complicated. I highly recommend people use a professional financial planner, but you should know that even that financial planner will ask you to be an active participant in the planning. Consider the person above that said he would get on a plane for $500 because that "might" be enough to find something he wanted to buy. He didn't have a $500 item he wanted to buy. He just assumed that at that large of a sum, there was likely something that would be worth getting on a plane. $500 was not the result of financial planning. It was likely the figure generated by someone who likely had never thought about financial planning.

You will get old

Getting old is inevitable. Here are the things that can and will happen to you as you age that will have a tangible impact on your finances:

- Your parents will die. If they have any part of taking care of you now, including giving you financial advice, that will fall to you. Even if they have a lot of money set aside for you, you will still have to manage it. If you are currently working, it is possible that your parents, before they die, might feel less need to provide for you financially since you are technically able to provide for yourself. This means that either your parents have left you the money you will have to manage, or they did not leave you money, and you will have to manage. Either way, you must manage money, so you had better start now.

- When people get old, they usually want to work less. Working 40 hours a week for 40 years is a lot of work. Sixty-seven may seem like an arbitrary age, but it's the average age in this country where we decided to start working less. You will need to manage your money well right now to have a chance to slow down your working at age 67. Again, I don't recommend stopping work altogether for the average 67-year-old, but you must have spent and saved your money intentionally and wisely to have a chance at working less.

- As you age, your body ages. As a result, older people have more chances of getting sick and impaired. There might come a time you are unable to work. If you have not managed your money to that point, this could create a serious hardship for you. Also, the longer you live, the more chances you have to become sick or otherwise disabled. If you go to the doctor yearly for a checkup (which I highly recommend), you should also manage your money. Both activities work together to prevent avoidable tragedies and hardships.

- The alternative is the government. Some people tell me they believe that when their parents die, it will be ok since the government will step in to care for them. Even though there is some truth to this, I assure you that the quality of care you get from the government will be nothing like what your parents gave you. No one I know chooses to be cared for by the government. Those I talk to who are cared for by the government mostly wish it were otherwise. The point is that you can make decisions today that decrease the likelihood of the need for government assistance in the future. Do not let lack of interest or future planning be the line that divides financial independence from government reliance.

Accidents and Emergencies

Accidents and emergencies are things that happen to other people until they happen to you. The longer I live, the more attuned I have become to how commonplace accidents and emergencies are. We indeed build social structures, like friend groups and families, to support us in our time of need. But financially, we have a lot of industries built on helping people through unexpected tough times. Insurance is probably the primary industry to address unexpected tragedies from a financial perspective. Health insurance might be the most common, but we also have social security, auto insurance, and a host of other major and minor insurances to cover tragedies. Our insurance industry is so large that many think it has subtly eroded local humanitarian responses to disasters. For instance, it was commonplace for aging adults to live with adult children in the past. Now we have nursing homes that are primarily paid for by insurance and subsidized by the government. Insurance is so standard as a solution for dealing with emergencies that some insurances are mandated, such as auto and homeowners insurance. Health insurance also used to be mandated in this country and may be again someday. If you do not know how much money is in your bank account, you likely do not know much more about your insurance and other safety nets designed to deal with unexpected tragedies and emergencies.

Savings pay for retirement

I have stated elsewhere that retirement is a huge industry. Some professionals help you plan it, and others help you live it. For the most part, the plan in the US is for retirement to be paid for by people's savings. Different retirement calculators will estimate how much you need to save to live your life. Almost all of these calculators you find online will give you a set amount you need to save every month until you retire to live this kind of life. The point is that you must save now for something that happens decades from now. There is no other way to pay for it other than through your savings, and very few people have the money lying around without saving ahead to retire and live a good life.

There's nothing I want to buy

Here is the challenge in working with people who say there's nothing they want to buy: not everything you need is something you want right now. Most people who tell me there's nothing they want to buy are thinking about what they want to do this evening. "There's nothing I want or need to entertain myself this evening" is a better way to word their response. Some people will look forward to the weekend and recall they have a video game with 100 hours of play left on it and say there's nothing they want to buy. When parents ask their child in my office, "Isn't there anything you want to buy?" it would be better for them to say, "Wouldn't you like to have money for impulse spending?" Rephrasing the question that way would at least get everyone on the same page, even if it's not exactly what the parent means. We must have a future focus when thinking about income and spending.

The point is that there are things people want and need, good things that require saving money and financial planning. Here are some:

- **A car**. Most people need a car to get to work. Most people who do not have a vehicle have to make compromises in where they work. Such compromise is especially true for low-wage workers. A car is a limiting factor for many people who want to advance their careers or make more money. People indeed take loans to buy cars, but not all people qualify for a car loan. A vehicle also requires ongoing maintenance, which costs money.

- **A house**. Rent or the expenses of maintaining a place to live is usually the single most significant portion of the working adult's living expenses. One way people afford to retire is to purchase a house, so they no longer have to pay rent. A house also is a commodity that appreciates over time (i.e., it gets more valuable over time). Even though most people take loans to buy a house, a down payment is required, usually about 20% of the total value of the house. Home loans (i.e., mortgages) typically take 15-30 years to pay off, just in time for retirement for most people.

- **Marriage**. The ceremony does require money, but that's not the point of this paragraph. If you have no money due to failure to plan, it can be hard to find people to marry you who you want to marry. This problem used to be true just for men, but now it is more true for women as our society becomes more egalitarian. Courting a spouse (dating) is also extremely expensive. Maintaining a social life is costly. Finding your marriage partner, from going out casually with friends who eventually introduce you to someone and you end up marrying that someone, costs a lot.

- **Education**. After high school, education costs a lot of money. There are indeed loans for education, but while you're in school, you are not working. And you still have to live. Getting an advanced degree takes a considerable amount of financial planning. It's why there are financial planners at colleges that help you figure out how you're going to pay for everything after you're accepted to the college. What if you have a career and then want to go back to school to train further or for a new job? If you're not already well-versed in essential financial planning, you will find returning to school a tremendous financial challenge. Sometimes, it may be why you never pursue a new career or get a better job.
- **Children**. You can't even manage your own finances, and now you must manage the finances of a whole other person-a person who is financially dependent on you?
- **Retirement**. Like I said, if you haven't been planning financially for retirement for at least a couple of decades, forget about it.

How your spartan lifestyle will work for you

One of the biggest problems of the individual spender in this country is over-spending. People routinely spend more money than they have. To many of my clients, this makes no sense. Having this thought is beneficial, though, because just doing what makes sense to you in the area of not spending more money than you make and not buying things you don't need will help you avoid one of the biggest financial pitfalls in modern society.

If you take a moment to look at the literature, videos, and podcasts on financial planning for the average person, most of them will be talking about over-spending. If you do not overspend or even understand why someone might, you can skip over at least half of the advice. Instead, you will likely learn a lot from researching our "debt-based economy." Not all debt is bad. There is such a thing as "good debt." Your research will likely challenge your thinking about finances, but it will be worth it, so please do it.

Another quality, the living-in-the-moment kind, is also beneficial to financial planning because long-term investment advisors counsel us to take a portion of our paychecks and deposit it directly into an investment account where compounding interest is the engine. Then forget that it's there. Even a small amount of money over long periods (e.g., the decades before your retirement) will generally result in significant returns on your investment. Since money has little meaning or significance to most of my clients, taking a little from your check and putting it into an investment account to sit there for decades is a small sacrifice for most of them.

Finally, most of my clients live lives of simplicity. Asceticism is a philosophy, religion, or simply a way of life. Ascetics shun indulgences and live disciplined lives of self-sacrifice. Most of my clients achieve similar results but without discipline and self-sacrifice. This situation is good because, as I said above, we live in a materialistic culture that makes it easy for people to spend more money than they have. Indulging is not always bad, but I think we waste a lot of money on things we only enjoy temporarily. We buy things we don't need and don't even like all the time. Imagine how much money we would have to work with if we just stuck to buying what we needed and living a simple life. Most of my clients are already there, so finding money in the budget to save is typically very simple.

That's the primary message for this chapter. Smartly managing your finances will be a challenge in regards to the act of planning, but lifestyle-wise, it should be pretty simple for most. The key, though, is to do it.

What needs to be managed?

Listed here will be the basics of a financial plan. I want to be clear that I am not a financial planner and don't have a degree in business or finance. I am a regular guy who has had to manage personal and business finances, though. I have discovered that finances can get very complex if you want them to be. More complex does not always mean better, though. Also, there is a host of good, free advice on essential finances that will get you started and help you ask the questions where you'll need professional advice. However, getting professional guidance through a certified financial planner is wise. Here are the basics.

Banking

You should have a checking and savings account at a bank. Your bank accounts are the portal through which all your money is funneled. Your job will deposit your paycheck into your checking account, and you will withdraw or transfer money from your checking account to pay bills and save money. Most banking happens through the internet; even if there is a "brick and mortar" bank one can visit to talk with a banker. However, most of my clients like having a phone number they can call and ask questions, so a bank with a physical location in your neighborhood might be the best option. You should also know how to access your account online. You may gain access from a computer, your phone, or both. Without this ability, it will be difficult for you to pay for anything. As I said above, the biggest challenge for most of my clients in accessing their accounts online is remembering their passwords.

Credit

Learn about credit because we have a debt-based economy. For most purchases, we borrow money from a bank and then pay the bank at the end of the month. Such transactions are what a credit card is for. For larger purchases, like appliances, cars, and houses, we take longer to pay the bank back and borrow the money with interest. Interest is the bank charging you money to use their money. These are usually called "loans," but buying a car with a credit card is possible. I would highly recommend against this because the interest on credit cards (which the bank charges you if you do not pay them back at the end of the month) is enormous. A friend of mine once paid for college with a credit card. It took him years and thousands of dollars in interest to pay back the bank. Do not do this.

Every person has a credit score. A credit score is a number from 300 to 850 that banks use to decide what kind of risk (i.e., whether or not you will pay them back) they are taking to loan you money. Higher scores mean lower risk. This information is essential because the higher your risk (i.e., lower credit score), the more the banks charge you to borrow money. People don't get higher scores by not using credit, though. No credit use history is almost as bad as poor credit history (i.e., low credit score). You must use credit (i.e., borrow money) and pay it back on time, all the time, for your credit score to go up. Again, a high credit score can save you a lot of money when borrowing money to buy a house (i.e., a mortgage).

Investment

Investing is different than saving. The point of saving money is to have it available for a later purchase. The end of investing money is to give it to someone to use so that they will pay you back later with interest. Even though banks have savings accounts that pay interest (after all, the bank is using your money while it's sitting in the account--that's what banks do), that interest is usually lower than the inflation rate. The result is that your money might become less valuable over long periods. If you want to save money to use at a future date (e.g., a year or more in the future), you should invest it. A typical bank savings account might pay you a tenth of a percent to one percent (.10%-1.0%)

interest to use your money. Most investment accounts aim to deliver their clients about 7%. That's a huge difference, and as I said above, it is the difference many times between saving money that pays for retirement or not. When investing money, I recommend people consult a financial planner. Investment can get complicated fast, and a lot of people would like to take advantage of you. Financial planning is a regulated industry that will provide you with some safeguards in your investment choices.

Budgeting

A budget is a detailed description of how much money is coming in and going out. The coming-in part is usually people's pay from work. The going-out part is usually people's expenses or things they buy. One can manage a budget in many ways, but most people find a spreadsheet the easiest way to manage a budget. But why do people create budgets? Budgets give people the data they need to plan. Budgets do not solve our financial issues. Budgets give us the information we use to solve financial matters. Even children can create budgets. I like doing budgets with kids because it is usually straightforward. We write down how much money they get each week for their allowance, and then we split the money in half with my patented 50/50 Plan. Half is for spending, and half for saving. So, if a child gets $2 a week, they can spend $1 and save $1 each week. At the end of the month, they have saved $4. An adult's budget is usually much more complicated. Even the young adult that lives at home but has a full-time job has multiple expenses. Each expense has its condition of payment. For instance, a young adult might have to pay for transportation (e.g., car, gas, bus), a cell phone, and entertainment. Entertainment is a big category for people, so that item in the budget needs to be "itemized" or made into several things such as food, movies, and video games.

The point of the budget is less about creating categories and more about being able to account for every cent that gets acquired and spent on a routine (usually monthly) basis. I have to admit that I do not like creating budgets. I quickly discover that my drive to be specific and thorough can make the whole activity very laborious and unsatisfying to me. This dilemma happens mostly because my finances, as a married parent running my own business, are relatively complicated. As a result, I spend a considerable amount of time monthly tracking my income and expenses so I can make financial decisions.

There are many free and paid resources to help people with budgeting, so websites like mint.com and others have developed ways to help people create and manage budgets. Unfortunately, these websites still require considerable time to set up and maintain. However, my budget is the main thing that keeps me from financial ruin in the short term. Indeed, any financial planner you meet with asks if you have a budget and, if not, helps you create one. In my opinion, all adults need to have a budget. My budget is also the first thing I will consult when there is a change to my income or expenses. Many people I talk to have to guess about being able to afford something or make plans for the future. Budgets allow you to eliminate guessing and make planning possible.

Final words about finances

We have a very peculiar relationship in this country regarding financial education. Some children receive financial education as part of their compulsory education. Others might learn about finances in math, politics, government, or history classes. I have found that classical education, especially college-preparatory (so, high academic achievers), does not usually teach formal financial education. Traditionally, the mid to lower-achievers seem to get the financial education that would benefit all people. However, even this education is inadequate in most cases I have observed.

There is a wealth of free information available on finances. You will notice that most adults you ask have at least a basic knowledge of finances. Typically, the adults I surveyed say that they got this information from their parents, not necessarily through formal education. Of course, some people study finance in college, but among those that do not, it seems that financial education comes primarily from within the family. For this reason, you will notice that many friends might give financial advice based more on their values than on facts. For instance, some people I talk to believe that using credit is always wrong, so they have no credit cards and do not take loans, and how they structure their finances will reflect that belief about credit. Their advice will be good for you depending on how closely your values match their values and not necessarily on how sound the advice is.

In this country, we tend to combine finances and morality. This tendency might explain why financial education is not standard academic coursework in the formative education system. You might notice that much of the financial literature is produced by religious institutions or individuals who use religion as a framework for financial advice. I believe this is the result of a conflation of finances and morality. I am bringing this up for several reasons. First, people need to be careful about the type of financial advice they receive. It makes sense to ask a religious institution for guidance if you want to know how to spend money morally. If you would like to know how to spend money smartly, you might want to consult a non-religious institution. By the way, a person's stated religious background (or lack thereof) does not mean they are necessarily giving good, law-abiding advice. Nor does it mean they are providing advice with pure intentions. I recommend people be very selective about the advice they seek and the source giving the advice. Again, financial planning is a regulated industry, so licensed individuals have an extra layer of scrutiny on their financial advising designed to keep the public safe.

Finally, formative financial education seems to be taught the old-fashioned way—from one generation to the next—within families. I think it makes sense to find someone you know that has a good track record of managing their money and giving good advice and ask for help with financial planning. They may teach you basic financial education, or they may refer you to the person they go to for financial advice. This person will be an excellent place to start for most people who find themselves at the beginning of the process of financial planning.

Conclusion

The high un/underemployment rate for individuals on the spectrum, and especially high-functioning individuals on the spectrum validates the existence of this book.   When I am diagnosing the problem of un- or underemployment I look at two broad categories: will and skill.

Will

Does my client want to work?   Are they committed to applying effort over time for a future reward?   Eugene Peterson, an American Presbyterian pastor and writer called discipleship, "a long obedience in the same direction."   This has always struck me as an appropriate description of someone's career.   Often when someone is out of work or otherwise failing to be productive by society's standards, we focus attention on the person's willingness to work or to push themselves. We see waking up late, achieving minimal expectations, having little care for the hustle and bustle of the outside world as a sign of laziness. People conclude my clients would rather lay in bed all day than "carry their own weight." They are called freeloaders, among other things.

I have discovered many un- or underemployed people struggle with low motivation.   Rather than being a consequence of some moral shortcoming, however, low motivation seems more often the result of persistent hardship and failure.   If nothing you did resulted in much, or if the effort it took to get someplace good seemed inordinate, why apply any effort at all?   If I was moving my family west in a covered wagon and watching people wiz by me in sports cars, I would likely stop and build a house right there.   Low motivation, or lack of "will" is absolutely a problem in my work with individuals on the spectrum when it comes to all sorts of things, and especially joining the workforce.   Rather than a moral shortcoming, however, I typically discover that life is simply "too hard" or the effort required "not worth it" for many people, and my job becomes making life more "doable" through advocacy, education, accommodation, and skill development.

Skill

My Behaviorist graduate school supervisor used to ask this simple question when beginning any sort of evaluation or intervention, "Can they even do the thing you're asking them to do?" For instance, when coaching parents on toilet-training she would mention the fact that using the bathroom included at least 14 distinct behaviors and each of those behaviors could be further broken down into their own discrete behaviors. The point was that toilet training was no simple task yet we get frustrated and describe them as "stubborn" when toddlers take longer than a few days to train. Hopefully I have made the case in this book that learning how to work, including getting and keeping a job and working that job for a long time, is an incredibly difficult task that will take time and effort to learn, and additional time to master. Traditional educational systems address this skillset in a way, but for people with different learning needs, that method is usually insufficient.

This is not to say that my clients cannot learn. Quite the opposite, in fact. Most testimonials I hear from employers report that a sufficiently and patiently trained autistic employee is an asset to the business. They are described as pleasant, dependable, and honest. My clients have also used their over-developed ability to hyperfocus and obtain specialties to perform very unique and necessary tasks for businesses. They become invaluable employees and achieve raises and promotions.

In the way that most of my clients took longer to learn to walk or speak, they take longer to learn to work. Despite the difference in course of learning, the outcome is always they same. Namely, they learn. They get it, even if it seems to take longer than it should. But "longer than it should" is a biased and subjective assessment and meaningless once the skill is achieved. Ask any parent of a child that took "longer than he should have" to toilet train if they are not overjoyed that their child is toilet trained.

This book is not exhaustive of all of the skills it takes to have a long, successful career, but my belief is that it is sufficient to get someone moving in the direction of work, and sustain them over a long obedience of productivity.

www.ingramcontent.com/pod-product-compliance
Lightning Source LLC
Chambersburg PA
CBHW060046260726
48658CB00004B/1205